Zeus Syndrome

Zeus Syndrome: A Very Short History of Religion-Based Masculine Domination is a critical assessment of the biblical concepts of gender hierarchy and the intersection of sex/gender, power, and religion.

Starting with #MeToo and the abuse of religious power in the Catholic Church, it also presents a concise selection of historical case studies. In doing so, the book demonstrates how a specific construction of the relationship between sex/gender, power, and religion not only excludes women and every person conceived as feminine or effeminate from power but also produces – almost automatically – a rape culture, which uses and excuses violent sexuality as an appropriate manifestation of masculine power.

Biblical studies is increasingly interdisciplinary and frequently focuses on contextualising the reading of biblical texts. This volume focuses on how:

- The Bible is intertwined with other religio-cultural traditions in the Mediterranean world.
- Biblical and extra-biblical ancient concepts of gender hierarchy have left traces in the cultural memory, particularly of the Western world.
- The Bible is received and applied in the contemporary world, above all in the politics, news media, and churches of Western post-Christian societies and African Christianity.

Throughout this text, religious history and biblical tradition are linked with recent conflicts to show how traces of these concepts continue to resonate and influence the world of today even in post-Christian societies.

Joachim Kügler is a Professor of New Testament Studies at University of Bamberg, Germany.

Rape Culture, Religion and the Bible
Series Editors: Caroline Blyth, *University of Auckland, New Zealand*
Johanna Stiebert, *University of Leeds, UK*

Resisting Rape Culture
The Hebrew Bible and Hong Kong Sex Workers
Nany Nan Hoon Tan

The Bible and Sexual Violence Against Men
Chris Greenough

Rape Culture, Purity Culture, and Coercive Control in Teen Girl Bibles
Caroline Blyth

Trafficking Hadassah
Collective Trauma, Cultural Memory, and Identity in the Book of Esther and in the African Diaspora
Ericka Shawndricka Dunbar

Vocation and Violence
The Church and #MeToo
Miryam Clough

Zeus Syndrome
A Very Short History of Religion-Based Masculine Domination
Joachim Kügler

For more information about this series, please visit: https://www.routledge.com/Rape-Culture-Religion-and-the-Bible/book-series/RCRB

Zeus Syndrome
A Very Short History of Religion-Based Masculine Domination

Joachim Kügler

LONDON AND NEW YORK

First published 2023
by Routledge
4 Park Square, Milton Park, Abingdon, Oxon OX14 4RN

and by Routledge
605 Third Avenue, New York, NY 10158

Routledge is an imprint of the Taylor & Francis Group, an informa business

© 2023 Joachim Kügler

The right of Joachim Kügler to be identified as author of this work has been asserted in accordance with sections 77 and 78 of the Copyright, Designs and Patents Act 1988.

All rights reserved. No part of this book may be reprinted or reproduced or utilised in any form or by any electronic, mechanical, or other means, now known or hereafter invented, including photocopying and recording, or in any information storage or retrieval system, without permission in writing from the publishers.

Trademark notice: Product or corporate names may be trademarks or registered trademarks, and are used only for identification and explanation without intent to infringe.

British Library Cataloguing-in-Publication Data
A catalogue record for this book is available from the British Library

Library of Congress Cataloging-in-Publication Data
A catalog record has been requested for this book

ISBN: 978-1-032-21229-6 (hbk)
ISBN: 978-1-032-21551-8 (pbk)
ISBN: 978-1-003-26997-7 (ebk)

DOI: 10.4324/9781003269977

Typeset in Times
by KnowledgeWorks Global Ltd.

To Ragies and his family!

Contents

	Acknowledgements	ix
	Introduction	1
1	A Female King? The Public Body of Hatshepsut	13
2	Hatshepsut Baptised: Christian Women as Sons of God	32
3	Why One Must Not Turn a Man into a Woman (Egypt – Greece – Rome)	49
4	Defending Masculinity Under Oppression: The Biblical Plan to Be Different	68
5	The Beautiful Ruler and the Ugly Redeemer	84
6	"God-Wives", "Old Virgins", "Young Widows": Women Without Human Husbands	103

7 Zeus-Syndrome, #MeToo, and the Hope
for Something New 120

Bibliography 126
Index 135

Acknowledgements

According to a popular German saying, "success has many fathers". Yet, in the case of this book, it is more about "many mothers" of success.

I am so grateful for the unwavering support of my secretary (and sometimes saviour) Irene Loch, who is so effective in solving problems and navigating administrative challenges. Without her, it would not have been possible to write this book in times of a pandemic, remote teaching, home office, and all the new regulations and duties that arose during an academic "state of emergency". I wish to thank my student helper Karelle Eyafa, who impressed with her reliability, intelligence, and high-speed work. Additionally, I am grateful for the funding of the Alexander von Humboldt Foundation, which allowed me to host a number of high-ranking African scholars at my university: among them, Masiiwa Ragies Gunda, Musa W. Dube, Rosinah Gabaitse, Lilly Phiri (†), Ezra Chitando, Lovemore Togarasei, Kudzai Biri, Molly Manyonganise, Mmapula Diana Kebaneilwe, and Louis Ndekha. In large part, this book is a result of an academic discourse on gender, power, and religion they initiated and maintained over years. I learned so much from you: thanks!

Above all, I have to express my deepest gratitude to Johanna Stiebert, who had the most impact on my work. After reading my first book[1] on the topic (Kügler 2021), she had the idea of me authoring this one, critically and helpfully accompanied the whole process of writing, and transformed my "Germenglish" into proper English. Thousand thanks!

x *Acknowledgements*

Finally, yet importantly, I thank Routledge Focus, for accepting my project for publication, and the editors (at the time of acceptance) of RAPE CULTURE, RELIGION AND THE BIBLE, Caroline Anne Blyth and Johanna Stiebert, for integrating it into this important series. I am grateful for the help coming from Barbara Thiede, one of the new editors. Her comments were more than welcome!

While I was working on this book, I often felt reminded of the German author Thomas Brasch (1945–2001), who keeps fascinating me since the 1980s, although I do not share his communist vision. He once talked about the contradictions "between the Old which is dead but powerful and the New which is vital but not in view" (Brasch 1982, my translation). My hope is that this book, by focusing on so many contradictions and transformations, will enable some of its readers to get the vital New into focused view.

Note

1 My German book *Sexualität – Macht – Religion. Zeitreisen ins Bermuda-Dreieck menschlicher Existenz* (2021) was the first step to explore the intersection of sexuality/gender, religion, and power. Although my German publisher Echter Verlag left the right of doing an English translation with me, this book is not a translation of the first one. While the German book addressed a public without deeper knowledge of religious studies, biblical studies, and ancient languages, this one gets much deeper into the academic discussion. In addition, I reordered the material, used different graphics, and introduced new theoretical framework for interpretation.

Introduction

Rape Culture – The Sociocultural Context of This Book

For more than a decade, the Roman Catholic Church, still the biggest global player in World Christianity, has been shattered and scattered by scandals of sexual abuse again and again. In the countries involved, like the USA, Ireland, Chile, and Germany, Catholicism is experiencing a devastating loss of social authority and political influence. Many people, among them members and friends of the Church, ask what is the point or benefit of traditional Christian doctrine if it is not even able to immunise the inner circle of the Church against such evil things as child abuse and other forms of sexual violence. Instead of being a safe place for children and other vulnerable persons, we learn that church structures were and are used to protect perpetrators and blame victims. Moreover, the same doctrinal tradition that used to portray celibate priests as holy, flawless persons, living in perfect purity, seems to be of no help at all in dealing with the abuse crisis in a way that does justice to the victims or turns the church into a safe place for all.

Even worse, the Catholic Church is not the only culprit that global movements for sexual integrity as a basic human right are having to contend with. Sexual abuse seems to be everywhere, in other churches (cf. e.g. Chitando & Chirongoma 2013; Manyonganise 2016; Vengeyi 2016; Zimunya & Gwara 2019), as well as in almost every part of modern societies (Stiebert 2020).

DOI: 10.4324/9781003269977-1

The term "rape culture" is not simply a fashionable label created by radical feminists but an apt name for the culture we all are living in, as the #MeToo-movement, prominent among others, is showing again and again.

As a specialist of the New Testament and of related religious history in antiquity I am an expert of the past not of the present times. Therefore, the purpose of this book is not to deliver a handbook on how to deal with modern problems of violent sexuality. I do, however, try to make things clearer and easier to understand by highlighting the religio-historical patterns that structured "rape cultures" in the past and which resonate on into present times.

In many ancient cultures, the connection between sexuality and power is obvious in theory as well as in practice. Thus, a fresh look at these cultural traditions may help us to understand better how our own cultural systems are constructed, even if they tend to cover up the relationship between sexuality and power. Indeed, since the times of romanticism (i.e. the late 18th and most of the 19th century) we have tended to link sexuality more explicitly with love, rather than with power. And this attitude remains vivid and influential. When the hippie-movement of the 1960s, sharing in the "sexual revolution" of that time, produced the slogan "Make love, not war!" (although more likely 'have sex instead of making war!' was meant) the ideological basis of the slogan was the romanticist confusion of sexuality and love. The way in which modern societies tend to link sexuality with romantic love and deep emotion seems so strong that the numerous cases about sexual violence against children, women, men, and all others[1] are still interpreted as monstrous exceptions. What if child-abuse scandals in churches, the international #MeToo- and #MenToo-movement (cf. Greenough 2021: 8–18) refer to the monstrous symptoms of a general culture, which links sexuality predominantly with power? The analysis of the ancient concept of sexuality can serve as a tool for illuminating the relationship between sexuality and masculine power. This, in turn, can help in developing a more nuanced view of human sexuality with all its ambivalences, risks, and challenges. My intention here is not to regurgitate the traditional scepticism towards sexuality as something evil, which the Church inherited from certain ancient philosophers and carried forward. Instead, this book is meant as a contribution to an ethic of human sexuality, which is capable of integrating the dangerous sides of sexuality alongside the bright ones. Such an ethic understands sexuality as a creational gift that human beings can use for destructive ends but that can also be cultivated as an expression of intimacy, trust, and love.

Some Theoretical Clarifications

This book is not only a very *short* history of religion-based masculine domination but also a highly *selective* one. It is not my purpose to prove that all cultures at all times are structured as rape cultures. Instead, I focus on a few examples to show how specific ideological structures link sexuality with both power and religion, thus producing the fuel that keeps rape cultures running. This *structural approach* is different from a comprehensive cultural history of masculine domination and it needs only selected samples to make the few ideological basics of religion-based masculine domination visible and understandable. In this book, the way in which rape culture intertwines religion, power, and masculine sexuality is termed "**Zeus syndrome**". I coined this expression not only because it is more handy than "religion-based masculine domination" but also because in ancient times Zeus was not only the highest god of Hellenistic religions but also the prototype of a rapist, who treated human persons – men and women – as mere objects of his sexual desire and pursuit. In the figure of Zeus religion, power and sexuality become a unity: the toxic-sacred trinity of rape culture.[2] His divinity is exemplified by his power; his power is divine and also sexual, as it is displayed in acts of sexual violence that permit no limitation, be it by other deities, or by human beings. Zeus is the highest god and therefore the most powerful: thus, he can have sex with whomever he wants.

An important theoretical concept for my historical analysis is the idea of "**two bodies**". Usually, this idea is associated with Ernst H. Kantorowicz's famous book *The King's Two Bodies* (1957) and, of course, I owe much to his work. Yet, the concept of several bodies of one person is much older. Paul already uses it in his Apostolic Letters[3] that later formed the core of the slowly evolving canon of the New Testament. He sees the whole Church as the body of Christ and teaches that every single Christian is transformed into an incorporation of Christ by faith and baptism. This idea will be analysed in detail later on in this book. For now, it suffices to explain what I want to express when talking about different bodies and how this differs from Kantorowicz on the one hand and from Paul on the other.

- The term *personal body* refers to the physical body as the basis of individual life. Yet, *personal body* does not simply refer to the body's biological material. Instead, it captures the individual mind-concept of the biological body, which is a result of how the body's "owner" experiences, feels, and understands it. As human beings are socially formed, the personal body is always acted on by society, culture, religion, and other external influences. Thus, the personal body is not only a private concept, it is personal in the sense that it is the result of someone's individual mind-work reacting to the influences of religious, cultural, and other societal frameworks. Before the invention of high-quality mirrors and selfies the personal body was predominantly an inner image, while in modern times the many outside images of our bodies have to be integrated in our personal bodies. However, these new challenges for the specific mind-work of shaping the personal body did not really change the basic structure of the personal body as an individual image of our body which is influenced from outside.
- The *public body* already begins whenever our personal body is perceived by others, but it is much more than that. The public body more or less consists of the social role we want to or must play. Others' perception of our body is part of this role but not the biggest or most important one. The social role that someone is playing is the pivotal aspect of the public body, and it can be connected more loosely or more tightly to the personal body with its physical aspect. Sometimes in this book, the term public body will be specified. Yet, I

Introduction 5

want to make clear that *social, religious, political,* or *cultural* body are not additional concepts. They signify only specific aspects of the public body that are relevant in particular contexts. That is helpful as the public persona of human persons may consist of very different aspects that may even be like different worlds. Our contact and exchange with others usually happens in different areas, like partnership, family, friends, workplace, religious group and church, media, or global public. The ways these different worlds are connected with each other or not is an important topic for sociological and socio-historical discussion. Yet, in this book it will not be possible to contribute substantially to this discussion, as ancient sources only seldom show more than some fragments of someone's world. Furthermore, my expertise is in religious history rather than sociology.

Below is an overview on how the different terms I will use are categorised and connected:

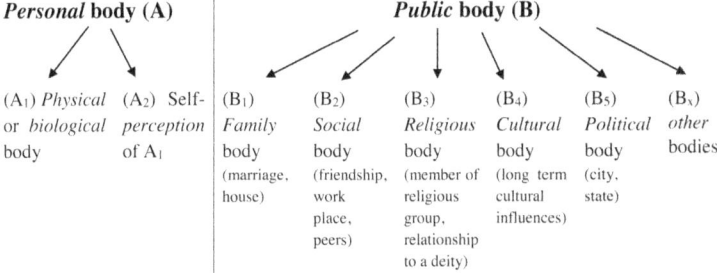

As already mentioned, this concept of multiple bodies has precursors in the Apostle Paul and the historian Kantorowicz, whose designation of "two bodies" has already experienced many variations of application (cf. Jussen 2009: 104). Focusing on the political role of the English king, Kantorowicz differentiates between a natural/mortal and a supernatural/immortal body. I open out this notion by claiming that with regard to every human person it makes sense to talk of several bodies. Although this book often focuses on public figures, such as kings and emperors, it will not suppose that only they have two bodies. Additionally, my theory is not primarily interested in the difference between supernatural vs. natural and immortal vs. mortal. These categories may play a role in some cases, but, if so, they are merely aspects of the more general difference between personal and public.

The difference between my body theory and Paul's use of the body lies in his limitation to the religious sphere. Instead, I use the term in a way, which is not limited to the religious sphere – even if religion plays an important role in this book. Furthermore, Paul uses the term "body of Christ" also in a collective way. Not only does the individual believer through baptism receive a messianic body as "Son of God" but also the whole congregation of believers constitutes the "body of Christ". This collective use of the body term does not play any role in my concept. However, what I learned from Paul is interest in the gender of the different bodies. Paul's question of how the gender of the personal and that of the religious body belong together remains important. Even if his answers and binaries may now seem outdated, Paul's interest in the question of how masculine the public body can be if one's personal body is feminine will serve as an eye-opener and may even help in answering the tantalising question about feminising the personal body by rape while the public body is powerful-masculine.

The Intersection of Sexuality, Power, and Religion

According to the doctrinal tradition of Christianity, religion and power belong together. God is understood as the supreme power, preached about and worshipped as the almighty ruler of all (Greek: παντοκράτωρ). For Judaism and Islam this is true also. The many gods of other religions may not be almighty, but, of course, they, too, are more powerful than human beings. Even if other aspects, like eternity or omnipresence, may characterise them as well, if higher power is not of their essence, they hold no religious importance. In the religious traditions analysed here, the intrinsic connection of divinity and power is incontestable. God/gods and power belong together. Thus, in the sources discussed here, religion is a tool of power, be it oppressive or liberating.

While the relationship between religion and power may not be that surprising for modern readers, the one between sexuality and power may be less apparent. As indicated above, this can be seen as one consequence of a certain romanticist confusion of *agape* (selfless love) and *eros* (desire/affection) in Western societies since the 19th century. Yet, social philosophers like Michel Foucault and Pierre Bourdieu brought back to the fore that sexuality and power in most cultural systems are tightly intertwined. Not that ancient societies in Egypt, Israel, and the Hellenistic-Roman world were necessarily aware of this relationship but, as we will see from the sources analysed below, the discourse was affirmative. As sexual rights were linked with the gender hierarchy in general, the rights of the father in the family, and of the ruler (and other powerful men) in society, sources from ancient Egypt, the Hebrew Bible and the Hellenistic-Roman world more often than not associate sexuality and power positively. Instead, Foucault (1978) and others discuss it in a critical way, insisting on the rights of women, children, and others. Ancient sources usually embrace male sexuality as a "natural" tool for exerting power. They see it as inevitable and acceptable that men dominate women – physically and symbolically. That is exactly what Pierre Bourdieu (2001 [1997]) – building on the ground-breaking study of Simone de Beauvoir (2011 [1949]) – recognises as the main achievement of patriarchy: namely, the capability of declaring the cultural technique of masculine domination as something natural.[4] While in modern times, nature is a secular term, it was linked with religion in ancient cultures. Because the cosmos was seen as divine creation, the internal structures of the universe, or natural laws, were also divine laws. And, with the social world of human society being part of the cosmic order, the divine laws of nature rendered the basic structures for human lives as for the non-human world. This idea is common for most if not all ancient cultures. It can be found in the old Egyptian concept of *ma'at* (cf. Assmann 1990; Quirke 1994; Assmann 2011), in sapiential tradition of the Hebrew Bible, the Septuagint, and the New Testament (cf. Dietrich 2019; Kyne 2021), and also in Platonism and Stoa, where the divine logos (cf. Tobin 1992: 348–349) are identified as the basic law of nature.

Thus, when we go back to the past we should keep in mind that the hiatus between nature and culture/religion so common in modern civilisations is scarcely applicable to ancient sources. Instead, we encounter cultural concepts where nature, religion, and society are thoroughly interwoven. This means that we should not be all too surprised when the sources we analyse often if not always conceive of the cultural ideas of gender roles and of the function and meaning of sexuality as something given by the divine order of creation.

The Logical Order of Chapters

The basic structure of this book is a chronological and thematic one. Every chapter centres on a discrete main source. This source's date of origin influences the placement of the chapter in the book. However, I have tried to avoid excessive repetition, hence the main sources are always linked to sources from other times and cultural contexts where a specific topic shows up in a comparable way.

I start with Hatshepsut, a female Egyptian king of the 15th-century BCE, and try to show how masculine domination is a cultural system that genders power. The example of Hatshepsut allows us to understand why powerful women need to masculinise their public body.

Audaciously jumping over one and a half millennia, the second chapter connects the Egyptian example with one in the New Testament. The Apostle Paul indicates in his soteriological teaching that Christian women experience a masculinisation of their public body in baptism as they become "sons of God in Christ". Thus, they gain the same position in the Church ("body of Christ") and share in ecclesiastical power without any gender-based discrimination.

The third chapter deals with the reciprocal process, the feminisation of men, which, in the cultural framework of masculine domination, is abominable and must be avoided by any man wanting power. Yet, it can be seen also that it may be attractive for powerful men to dominate other men like women. Here I start in around 1000 BCE with an Egyptian mythical narration on the power implications of male-male rape. Then, I follow this topic through different stages of development in Greece and Rome.

The fourth chapter focuses on a quite famous narrative of the Hebrew Bible, the story of Joseph and Potiphar's wife (Genesis 39). This story, most probably dating from Persian times, may help us to understand how slave-holding can disturb patriarchal gender-hierarchies. The chapter contextualises the topic of masculinity under threat with another prominent text within the Hebrew Bible, namely the prohibition of male-male-penetration in the book of Leviticus. Although the specific texts traditionally are used for condemning homosexuality, it becomes clear that these texts have more to do with the challenge of maintaining masculinity under the pressure of occupation and religio-cultural colonisation.

The fifth chapter contextualises the topic of masculine beauty with a few other texts to indicate the topic's range of variety within the Hebrew Bible and contrasts the tradition of masculine power-beauty with that of an ugly and powerless redeemer. The chapter deals with the gender symbolism of crucifixion, a death sentence meant to kill the delinquent not only physically but also to annihilate the crucified man's honour by feminising his public body. Thus, Christianity is dealing with a saviour whose public body is feminine. Some New Testament texts can help us understand how the masculinity of Jesus was re-established and how also his masculine beauty was restored by means of the resurrection message.

For the sixth chapter the main source is a text about widows from the first Epistle to Timothy, a pseudo-Pauline letter dating from the end of the 1st-century CE or even later. The way the text struggles with the topic of young women who avoid patriarchal marriage indicates that, in Christian congregations of the time, the institution of widowhood was a vehicle for women's independence. Christian widowhood, it appears, offers an attractive status because it not only reduces the oppressive influence of masculine domination on the widow but also invites her to share in the power of her heavenly husband. In contextualising this concept of marriage avoidance, some historical aspects of female religion-based singlehood are indicated, using examples from old Egypt, and early Jewish writings. These examples may highlight also the ambiguity of women's singlehood. Although the solitary life can be a means of liberation, it can also be an expression of masculine domination.

Finally, the closing chapter (Chapter 7) offers some tentative links to the present.

The Position of the Author

It is only fair to inform readers how I, the author, am connected with the topic at hand. As an ordained priest of the Catholic Church, I am part of a powerful religious system that discriminates against women; for example, by excluding them from ordination to the priesthood. And yet, this is only the most visible misogyny in my Church. A far greater problem is that my Church's doctrine and practice are soaked in a tradition that participates in the system of masculine domination. The sexual abuse scandals revealed in recent years indicate that there are violent sexual practices within the Church that directly and widely apply, foster, and facilitate rape-culture attitudes. Moreover, the traditional teachings of my Church are sceptical and negatively inclined to sexuality more generally. As a man, a theologian, and a priest, I am very unhappy with the sinful, misogynist status quo in both Church and society; not least, because being in the centre of an obviously sinful system marks me a sinner, too. Yet, my position also implies an advantage. If you decide to shoulder the obligation of celibacy given by the Church, you decide in a way to make sexuality a permanent topic in your life. Every priest, no matter if he defines himself as heterosexual, homosexual or other, no matter if living in accordance with the Church's norms always, sometimes, or seldom, is in a permanent discourse with others and with himself on sex, gender, and sexuality. People often ask, "why do you live that way?" – and you have to answer. They ask, "why are women excluded from priesthood?" – and you have to answer. "Why are priests disproportionately often involved in sexual abuse?" You have to answer. In addition, the questions

Introduction 11

of others are the same as your own, unless you benumb your critical self-consciousness with some traditional ideology. With time, I was able to understand that being exposed like this may sometimes feel like a curse but for a critical theologian it is a privilege as you are forced to reflect more deeply. Unprotected reflection tells me what I am. I am not only part of masculine domination in general,[5] but I am, in a specific way, at the centre of it. Thus, my critique of masculine domination is a kind of self-destruction. Yet, I trust that this kind of "suicide" is a redemptive one "because anyone who has died has been liberated from sin" (Romans 6:7).

Notes

1 Although I support the LGBTQ+ movement, I try to avoid the term in my book as I find it difficult to define properly the differences between men, women, children, and LGBTQ+. Instead I use the idiom "all others" to refer to persons of all genders and sexes that would not label themselves as man or woman.
2 It is fascinating to see how in the history of European art most artists know how to belittle the rape actions of Zeus. Almost no painting shows the horror or pain of rape victims. Hence, Ganymede in most paintings looks rather "surprised" when raped by the god, with no rejection, resistance, outrage, pain, or disgust visible (cf. "The Rape of Ganymede" (1636–1638) by P. P. Rubens; https://upload.wikimedia.org/wikipedia/commons/7/7a/Ganyrubn.jpg [accessed 13/04/2022], where the bared buttocks of the raped youth are already symbolically penetrated by arrows from a phallus-shaped quiver). The great Rembrandt seems to be the notable exception. In his painting of the same topic (1635) there is nothing majestic about the eagle; there is no heavenly light, no beautiful youth silently submitting to rape, just a crying baby, trying to escape the grip of the rapist and urinating in terror (cf. https://www.the-artinspector.com/post/rembrandt-ganymede [accessed 13/04/2022]).
3 Historical criticism tends to regard only seven letters in the New Testament as originally written by Paul (namely, Romans, 1 & 2 Corinthians, Galatians, Philemon, Philippians, 1 Thessalonians). The authorship of the other six writings in the New Testament associated with the name of Paul remains disputed and these epistles should be left aside when discussing the teaching of the historical Paul.

4 Below, we will encounter this naturalisation of a cultural technique in several cases. It can be found already in an Egyptian text on the contest between Horus and Seth (see Chapter 3), although Plato and his school made the most explicit statements on the "natural" character of masculine domination.
5 Bourdieu (2001 [1997]) explains that masculine domination is a comprehensive cultural system that involves all persons that live under its influence. Masculine domination, although privileging men, turns persons of any gender into its accomplices. Yet, there are, of course, differences in the way people reproduce, enforce, accept, or criticise this system.

1 A Female King?
The Public Body of Hatshepsut

The old Egyptian culture is not, most probably, the most misogynist one in the ancient Near East. And yet, it was clear that the king of Egypt[1] must be a man. The case of Hatshepsut,[2] of a woman being king, is an exception in Egyptian history – although not the only one. If we want to understand the challenges facing a woman on the royal throne, we have to look first at the mythical concept of Egyptian kingship, which delivered the political, cultural, and religious framework for Hatshepsut's reign.

The Gender of Power: The King as Man

The gender of Egyptian kingship is deeply rooted in the Horus myth, which provides the religious foundation. The royal myth of Osiris, Horus, and Isis identifies the king with Horus, the son who – supported by his mother Isis – takes revenge for his murdered father Osiris, thereby establishing justice.[3] As long as the king is alive, he sits on the throne, which symbolises Isis. "The association between Isis and the physical royal throne itself is perhaps indicated by the fact that her name may have originally meant 'seat', and the emblem that she wore on her head was the hieroglyphic sign for throne" (Shaw & Nicholson 2008: 159). Thus, the king as "living Horus" is, symbolically, seated on his mother's knees,[4] supported and upheld by her. The living king as the incarnation of Horus, the legitimate son and heir of Osiris, is male. As "Horus on the throne" he is also united with his mother and this union legitimates the rightfulness of his reign in accordance with *ma'at*, the divine world order.

At the same time, the king is also regarded as the son of the highest god Re (later united with Amun, the preeminent god of the New Kingdom, to become Amun-Re). For almost 3000 years, from Dynasty IV of the Old Kingdom until the time when Roman emperors ruled over Egypt, the king's title "Son of Re" (☉) is of highest importance. It combines with the king's proper name, thus linking his person to the highest god. The king, being son of the god, is reigning on the earth as divine representative, as a copy or reincarnation of Re, keeping the house of his divine father in proper order. Again, however, the role of a royal and divine *son*, be it the son of Osiris and Isis, or the son of Amun, presupposes both maleness and masculinity.

Opportunities and Obstacles: The Dynastic Context of Hatshepsut's Reign

The situation of the Egyptian kingdom in the 15th-century BCE was a critical one. When king Thutmose II died after a short reign, the heir to the throne, Thutmose III, was a little boy, unable to reign. Furthermore, the fact that his mother Isis was of low status in the harem of Thutmose II weakened his political position. On the other hand, the late king's principal wife, bearing the Egyptian title ḥmt nswt wrt ("Great Royal Wife") was Hatshepsut, but she had given birth "only" to a daughter, Neferura. Being of female sex excluded this child from succeeding her father Thutmose II to the royal throne.

However, the position of her mother was quite powerful, as Hatshepsut was not only the widow of Thutmose II but also the daughter of Thutmose I: she had been married to her half-brother. Sibling marriages were neither illegal, nor unusual for Egyptian royalty of this time. Such intra-dynastic marriages between royal children with different mothers maintained the elite status of the ruling family by excluding non-royal men. Thus, potential masculine rivals for the dynasty were kept away, while full sibling marriages (which might have been considered

A Female King? 15

incestuous) were avoided by integrating women from other families into the royal harem.

Anyway, it was Hatshepsut, the aunt and stepmother, who took over the role of vice-regent for her stepson and nephew, the child-king Thutmose III. Although we have no valid information on quite how and why she got this powerful post, it is highly probable that her strong dynastic position as royal widow and daughter of a king was the basis for her political career. It also appears to be the case that the boy-king's mother, Isis, was pushed aside and deprived of authority.[5]

After some years of ruling in the name of Thutmose III, Hatshepsut declared herself king. Such a step of extending her regency to full royal rule had to overcome two major obstacles. The first problem was that, with Thutmose III being king, the post was not available. Such a "lack of vacancy" would usually be resolved by murder. While an Egyptian king was a god and could not retire, he could be "passed on" to the other world by killing him. We do not know why Hatshepsut did not take this route. Instead, she found another solution for the problem. (We will look at this later.)

The second problem was much graver and more insoluble. As already indicated, ancient Egypt's royal ideology was entirely defined by the masculinity of the king. Royal mythology, titles, regalia, and typical images and patterns of royal texts – everything was gender-biased and subscribed to and assumed masculine domination. The king was "Son of Re", wearing clothes culturally defined as masculine, a ceremonial beard, and the tail of a bull hanging from the back of his royal kilt.[6] Although the tail-emblem, referring to the irresistible power of the king, lost some of its importance in later times, the corresponding royal epithets "Strong Bull", or "Mighty Bull", were used until the end of the Egyptian kingdom. In Roman time still, Titus Flavius Domitianus (Emperor 81–96 CE) used it on the obelisk he erected in Rome to glorify his reign.[7]

It is obvious, therefore, that the role of the king was thoroughly and unequivocally defined in masculine terms, leaving no room for a woman to take it on. Thus, it is not a surprise that the son of a minor royal wife, a young boy unable to rule, had taken over kingship from his father. Meanwhile, this course was closed to his half-sister Neferura, even though her mother Hatshepsut was the Great Royal Wife.

Nevertheless, Hatshepsut's status of principal wife of Thutmose II and daughter of Thutmose I made her position strong enough for her to become vice-regent for Thutmose III. In taking on this role, Hatshepsut had ousted the boy-king's lower-ranking mother Isis, even though the king's mother tended to be the most powerful woman at the royal court. Hence, it is Hatshepsut, not Isis, who, as vice-ruler for Thutmose III, is in official documents depicted as the woman adorned with the traditional regalia of a Great Royal Wife.[8]

Transformation: The Female Vice-Regent Becomes a King

Royal women acting as vice-rulers for a child-king did not unduly disturb the traditional system of Egyptian kingship. This is because the central role of power was held by a male and the female was, officially at least, acting "in the name" of the king. She was a kind of extension of the royal person, similar to the many royal officials in administration and religion. All of them acted "in the name" of the king, not in their own name and not "as king".

But, acting in her own name and as king was exactly what Hatshepsut tried to do. After some years – at the latest, after seven years – she decided to rule as king. Her royal name Maat-Ka-Ra shows that she claimed to rule as king according to *ma'at*, the religio-political order given by the gods. She solved the problem that Thutmose III was already installed as king by declaring *him* her vice-king with right of succession. This, however, necessitated a rewriting of recent history. Hatshepsut's husband, Thutmose II, was ignored. That opened the door for connecting Hatshepsut directly with Thutmose I who was now said to have installed his daughter as his successor. Following this (fictitious) model, Hatshepsut could then nominate Thutmose III as her successor and co-regent, joining her in kingship already during her lifetime. As such a construction was known already from the era of the 12th Dynasty (Middle Kingdom),[9] it could be argued to be a quite traditional one. At the same time, it can be seen as a very smart strategy. Labelling Thutmose III as co-regent avoided political murder *and* created a space for Hatshepsut's kingship in her own name, without depriving Thutmose III of his right to be heir to the throne.

The remaining "gender problem" was approached through a highly sophisticated double-pronged strategy. On the one hand, Hatshepsut worked on feminising the traditional concept of kingship, while on the other hand, she adapted her public body to conform to the traditional masculinity of the king. Given that texts and literary media generally are more flexible than visual images, Hatshepsut's attempts of opening up the mythological framework of kingship to feminine aspects are found most prominently in inscriptions associated with her. The process of adapting her political body to masculine gender norms of power, however, is more obvious in images of Hatshepsut, such as reliefs and statues of her.

While, as we will see, this distinction of literary versus pictorial is not absolute, all this is more plausible when we remember the high elasticity of gender (and other) concepts in texts, compared with the intransigence of images. Even nowadays, one would hardly use the pictogram of a person wearing trousers to identify a toilet for women, or, conversely, a skirt-wearing pictogram for the men's toilets. This is so, although in reality a high number of women wear trousers and in many regions men traditionally wear skirts, wraps, or dress-like shirts and robes. Cultural tradition in ancient Egypt had developed a specific stylisation for the royal image, regarding all of size, headgear, garment, sceptre, staff, facial characteristics, and gestures. This allowed for some variations but not regarding the gender of the ruler: the king was always represented as a man. Gendered aspects of royal iconography, consequently, made it difficult to integrate Hatshepsut's female sex into public[10] representations of kingship. Despite this, Hatshepsut devised some ways to represent herself as both king and woman, as some statues, found in the mortuary temple complex *Djeser Dejeseru* at Deir el-Bahari, may prove.[11] But, the overwhelming majority of reliefs and statues depicting her represent her as a man. Where Hatshepsut is shown in visual media together with her "co-regent" Thutmose III, only the names attributed to the figures make any gender distinction, not the pictures themselves (cf. e.g. Naville 1901: plate CV, left side).

The masculine iconography Hatshepsut adapted applies not just to dress and regalia. Rather, the royal body itself is rendered masculine. This can be seen clearly where Hatshepsut is depicted naked. In the famous relief series *Geburtszyklus* ("The Birth Cycle", see Brunner 1986) at Deir el-Bahari, Hatshepsut expresses her claim to be a true king according to the divine world-order of *ma'at* by showing her divine origin from Amun. The climax of this relief series, namely the scene where Amun presents Hatshepsut to the gods,[12] is the best example of radical gender adaption undertaken by Hatshepsut. While the text speaks of her as "daughter of Amun" the picture shows her as a naked[13] little boy standing on the knees of the divine father. The image of the naked divine child clearly shows a penis (cf. Kügler 2017: 118, fig. 4). Thus, Amun's child is visibly male, aligning with the traditional masculinity ascribed to all Egyptian kings.

This example of bodily masculinisation is of special importance, as it speaks against anachronistic (e.g. "transvestism") and psychological explanations of Hatshepsut's re-gendering. First, we do not know anything about the psychological disposition of Hatshepsut (or other Egyptian kings, for that matter) due to the formal character of the sources, which are, for the most part, highly formalised sacral or ceremonial documents. We also do not have any information about how Hatshepsut dressed privately. No paparazzi could snap her relaxing at the beach. Private sources we sometimes have access to nowadays (private letters, emails, diaries, ...) simply do not exist for Hatshepsut or any other Egyptian king. The private life was private in a strict sense. Secondly, it is also striking that masculinisation goes beyond using masculine royal garments, headgear, and other regalia: instead, in the images of this cycle Hatshepsut's *body is male*.

An adequate interpretation is best achieved when we call to mind the notion of the two bodies of a king (in this case, of Hatshepsut). The official royal documents show *the public body* of the king. This religious and political body is male as the role of the king is masculine. *The personal body* of Hatshepsut is not visible in these kinds of sources – not even where aspects of femininity are integrated (as mentioned above). Sure, the statues referred to earlier tentatively relate the public royal role of Maat-Ka-Ra to the female body of Hatshepsut, but they are not a representation of her personal body. At most, they allude to the female sex of this king, in some stylised or stereotypical manner. They say nothing, however, about what Hatshepsut's face or body really looked like: whether her breasts were big or small, whether she was tall or short, slim or fat, for example.

The concept of radical masculinisation of the public body may seem audacious, but it did not come out of nowhere. It is, instead, a continuation of the traditional differentiation between person and office, royal body, and personal body, which has been characteristic of Egyptian royal iconography going far back. Thutmose III is a little boy when he becomes king, but his royal body, visible in the official documents, is that of an adult man. If one of the Egyptian kings had just one eye or only three fingers on his right hand, we would not know about this. In royal iconography, *every* king is depicted according to the norms of an ideal man. The public body of *all* Egyptian kings is depicted as perfect, in line with cultural norms. The personal body is not depicted in royal documents. The purpose of such documents, after all, is not to describe reality but to create reality (cf. Assmann 1984: 108–112). Rhetorical and sacramental/magical in character, they are intended to establish an everlasting divine truth: this king is a true king according to *ma'at*; he performs the task of a king, and, therefore, his kingship will be eternal.

But, apparently, the personal body of the specific human being acting as king cannot be ignored completely. Sometimes this body must be explicitly acknowledged. This can be seen clearly when looking at Hatshepsut's House of Millions of Years, *Djeser Djeseru* at Deir el-Bahari, to which we turn next.

Daughter of a King

As mentioned above, written texts constitute a more flexible medium for the purpose of adapting or reconstructing royal traditions that might go some way towards acknowledging the sex and gender of Hatshepsut. While most images associate her with masculine royal iconography, inscriptions about Hatshepsut almost always indicate that the personal body of this king is female. It is not only that Hatshepsut's royal titles are feminised,[14] but elements of the mythological framework of kingship are also adapted to her sex. At least, one might say, she redefines the king's relationship to the divine along the lines of daughtership instead of sonship.

Three persons play an important role in Hatshepsut's mortuary temple at Deir el-Bahari: Amun and Thutmose I as fathers and Hathor as mother. These parent-daughter relations constitute the core of Hatshepsut's mytho-political strategy for legitimising her kingship. Consequently, they are prominent topics at Deir el-Bahari. This mortuary temple, like similar installations of other Egyptian kings, can be understood as an "eternity machine", designed for manifesting everlasting endurance ("millions of years") of a king's reign and posterity. To achieve this, the king has to proclaim that his kingship was in accordance with the divine world order *ma'at*, based on *ma'at*, and producing *ma'at*. As *Djeser Djeseru* also is an Amun temple, the mortuary cult of king Hatshepsut was linked with that of Amun to make the king of god and the god-king allies in the eternalising of each other's life-giving cult (cf. Kügler 1997: 69–71).

At first sight, the relationship to Thutmose I as a father might seem to be of less interest in this context than divine paternity, but this would give the wrong impression. First, being the daughter of king Thutmose I is one of the essential factors in Hatshepsut becoming king of Egypt. This dynastic status opens the door to power, first as vice-regent for Thutmose III and next, as king in her own right and name. Therefore, Hatshepsut presents her royal father as an important source of her legitimacy, stating, for instance, that her father himself destined her to be his co-regent and successor (cf. Shirun-Grumach 1993: 134–138). In an important relief at Deir el-Bahari (cf. Naville 1898: pl. LXI), one can see how Thutmose I, sitting on the royal throne based on *ma'at*,[15] presents his co-regent and successor Hatshepsut to the royal officials. While the iconography follows the norm of royal masculinity, depicting the public body of Hatshepsut as male, the inscription refers to the gender of the next king by using feminine nouns and pronouns. In his speech, Thutmose I admonishes the royal administration to strictly obey his daughter and he promises life to those obedient to her orders: "he who shall do her homage shall live, he who shall speak evil in blasphemy of her Majesty shall die" (Bryan 2000: 242).

The (albeit posthumous) construction of Thutmose I designating Hatshepsut his chosen successor suppresses the reign of Hatshepsut's half-brother and husband Thutmose II, effectively deleting him from history. Obviously, the relationship between daughter and father is ascribed much higher importance – politically as well as theologically – than the relationship between wife and husband, or sister and brother. Most probably, this has something to do with the polygynous character of royal marriages. Being one of the wives in the king's harem would not have provided requisite religio-political grounds for the claim to power, not even for a Great Royal Wife. Therefore, Hatshepsut "muffles" the kingship of her husband in favour of accentuating her direct kinship with her father, casting herself as his co-regent and immediate successor.

Daughter of a God

Compared with her royal father, Thutmose I, Hatshepsut's interest in her divine father Amun is much more considerable. Because her mortuary temple is, simultaneously, a temple for Amun, it is not a surprise that the relationship between father Amun and his daughter is the predominant topic in the manifold depictions of this huge cultic facility. The guiding theological idea, which determines the architecture, texts, and iconography of the temple at Deir el-Bahari, connects Hatshepsut's kingship with Amun king of gods in every way imaginable.

A central element of this programme is the "Birth Cycle" (*Geburtszyklus*, Brunner 1986),[16] the famous series of reliefs illustrating the king's divine origin. Amun is the one who begets Hatshepsut putting the child into the womb[17] of her royal mother Ahmose[18] (Naville 1896: pl. XLVII).[19] Khnum divinely creates the king (Naville 1896: pl. XLVIII, centre) and a huge number of goddesses assist and attend her birth (Naville 1896: pl. LI). Father Amun himself recognises her as the beloved daughter of his own body, taking her on his knees and nose-kissing his baby (Naville 1896: pl. LII). Goddesses as wet-nurses suckle Hatshepsut with divine milk (Naville 1896: pl. LIII), and therewith affirm and destine her to be king for eternity, according to the will of her father Amun and the divine world order *ma'at*.

Due to the special situation of Hatshepsut as female king, who pushes aside an existing (male) king, previous research has seen the main purpose of the Birth Cycle as political propaganda for Hatshepsut's kingship. Although this interpretation seems plausible on first view, it is not very strong, when we fully appreciate the character of our sources. First, Hatshepsut could only plan and construct this huge temple complex once she was already recognised as king and, therefore, able to control completely Egypt's state apparatus, with all the expertise, resources, materials, and work force necessary for a project of such dimensions.

And secondly, propaganda is designed to reach the largest and broadest audience possible. However, the texts and pictures at Deir el-Bahari were inaccessible to the vast majority of Egyptians. Already the name *Djeser Djeseru* ("Sanctuary-of-the-Sanctuaries") indicates that this place was strictly off limits to the profane world of ordinary people. Only a very small number of priestly experts could enter this most holy place.

And yet, in the Egyptian imagination, there was indeed a huge audience, if not a human one. It was *the community of gods and goddesses*, the divine world, which Hatshepsut wanted to address with her mortuary temple. Confirming her membership in the divine community is the primary message and purpose of this sanctuary. So, the specific function of the Birth Cycle is to stress that Hatshepsut is a legitimate part of the divine family, the true daughter of Amun. According to the divine order *ma'at*, she was indeed king, one who defeated chaos and efficiently kept it at bay.

Hatshepsut installed *Djeser Djeseru* for her father Amun, creating a realm full of treasures and pleasures appropriate to the king of the gods. Thus, through her supreme achievements, she demonstrated and earned that she was indeed a true child of Amun. Her mortuary temple complex focuses on this mytho-political claim as the consummate tribute and everlasting display of her kingship. Beyond death, the temple confirms, Amun and his daughter belong together. As a righteous king and true daughter, Hatshepsut is a manifestation of her father, and her reign a medium of his reign. It is for the sake of Amun that her kingship persists into eternity.

The aforementioned final scene (Naville 1898: plate LVI) of the cycle most clearly expresses the thorough orientation towards post-mortal existence as king in eternity. There, Amun presents his daughter to the community of deities. "Behold the daughter of Amun!" says the king of heaven to the gods. He keeps Hatshepsut (depicted as a naked royal boy) on his knees to express his fatherly relationship to the child. While in the parallel presentation scene with Thutmose I, the *human* administration is addressed and implored to full submission, here the *divine* world is addressed. The response of the deities, of course, is not obedience. Instead, as is more appropriate of deities, they confirm that the daughter of Amun truly is one of them. They ensure that Hatshepsut receives the eternal blessing, protection, and support from the whole divine pantheon. Her reign is affirmed as divine, her kingship as in accordance with the divine world order, *ma'at*. Therefore, it will last forever and ever.

Daughter of a Goddess

At Deir el-Bahari, Hatshepsut is depicted in relation not only to Amun, her divine father, but also to Hathor, her divine mother. The prominence of Hathor is partly in homage to local cultic traditions. The cultic veneration for Hathor, in her animal form of a wild cow, is a very ancient tradition in the desert valley of Deir el-Bahari. Furthermore, Hathor can also play the role of Isis, mother of Horus, therefore constituting an appropriate mother for a king who is conceived of as the "living Horus". Finally, one can speculate if a female king might have a special interest in associating herself not only with a male deity but also with a female one, representing bovine strength and, therewith, complementing, or offering an alternative to, the strong-bull-tradition.

While we cannot know which of these reasons was the most significant, it is obvious that Hatshepsut put special stress on Hathor, erecting an additional sanctuary for her divine mother (cf. Kügler 1997: 67–69). Jan Assmann (1982: 37) understands the chapel to Hathor as a monumental version of scene XII of the Birth Cycle: namely, the suckling of the king by divine wet-nurses. Although other topics also play an important role in Hatshepsut's chapel to Hathor, Assmann's proposal makes sense, as the king's iconic action of drinking divine milk from the udder of Hathor in her manifestation of a cow (Naville 1901: pl. CV) is of high prominence among the chapel's exquisitely crafted decorations.

The feeding scene is also of particular significance for Hatshepsut's royal legitimacy, as the divine milk transfers the essence of the divine mother.[20] As Hathor is identified as mother of Horus,[21] her feeding attributes and confers the qualities of Horus to her daughter-king Hatshepsut. This Horus-quality is both divine and royal, comprises legitimacy and power, and promises eternity: "My beloved daughter Maat-Ka-Ra, I am your mother, creator of your beauty (*neferu*).[22] I have nursed you, so that you have the rights of Horus, the royal power of the south and of the north. I give you years in eternity", speaks the divine mother to her (adult) suckling.

Other reliefs show how the Hathor cow is tenderly licking the hand of the king. The texts explain that with this sign of love and care royal-divine qualities are transferred from mother to daughter: divine odour, life, power, eternal reign, and happiness. Although iconography and texts of the Hathor chapel characterise the relationship between mother and daughter with lyrical tenderness, the purpose is a highly politicised one. The king is again integrated into the religio-political framework of the royal Horus myth, thus receiving a Horus-like kingship: legitimate, powerful, and eternal.

The genders of King Hatshepsut come into quite obvious conflict with the traditional gender of power. Just because Hatshepsut tries to retell the traditional royal myths in a way that pays some tribute to her female sex, the gender messages conveyed by this king are quite ambivalent. Being *daughter* of

Hathor, Amun and Ra, King Hatshepsut, is, at the same time, Horus, *son* of Isis/Hathor. After her death, she is transformed into Osiris, *father* of Horus, as can be seen in the numerous monumental Osiris-pillars at Deir el-Bahari.[23] Thus, the gender conflict is not only between the texts referring to her in feminine gendered terms and the images showing her royal masculinity. Inasmuch as the king's personal femaleness had to be integrated into the thoroughly masculine mythical role of male Horus (and Osiris), gender ambiguity can be found within the texts also.

Yet, this ambiguity is not a mistake; it is absolutely necessary for Hatshepsut. If she had failed to mention her female identity at all, her personal body would have vanished from the royal monuments, with severe consequences for her mytho-political purpose and posterity. Without her feminine name, Hatshepsut, and without mention of her personal body's femaleness, her eternal memory as king Maat-Ka-Ra, would have had an empty casing, devoid of Hatshepsut's personal body. Without mentioning the personal body of the king, the immortalising would refer only to the royal role and body, which was already eternal according to the Horus-Osiris-concept. Every king who wanted to achieve personal eternity had to integrate their personal body into the public body of the royal role that functioned as the divine casing for the individual king. Following this logic, Hatshepsut had no option. It was absolutely necessary for her to mention her personal name and to integrate her personal, female body into the religio-political shell of kingship. The gender ambiguity resulting from this was negligible compared with not being mentioned, not appearing in the royal role, and therefore, not sharing in royal eternity.

No Eternity for Hatshepsut: A Woman Is a Woman

Nowadays, we still know about Hatshepsut's reign. We are fascinated by the beauty of her monuments and cherish her as one of the most important kings of Egypt.[24] Thus, one could say that her eternity project was successful. From an Egyptian perspective, however, Hatshepsut failed to immortalise herself as a legitimate king-god. In her case, "eternity" lasted at most

20 years. Already shortly after her death a high-ranking official, Ahmose Pen-Nekhbet, did not acknowledge Hatshepsut's kingship in his mortuary monument (cf. Grimm & Schoske 1999: 32), although he claims to have functioned as the tutor of Neferura, Hatshepsut's daughter.[25] Under the reign of Thutmose III, the destruction of Hatshepsut's monuments began, and her reign was ignored in the official lists of kings (cf. Schneider 1994: 130 and 132; Grimm & Schoske 1999: 30–31).

We do not know exactly the reasons for the *damnatio memoriae* overshadowing Hatshepsut's kingship, but we can be sure that her gender had something to do with it. Joyce Tyldesley (1996: 190, fig. 7.3) mentions a pornographic graffito which – together with other humiliating graffiti found in the area of Deir el-Bahari – may indicate that even ordinary men dared to express their rejection of and disdain for Hatshepsut and her reign. The vulgar graffito shows a worker or overseer having sexual intercourse from behind with a woman wearing royal headgear. Most probably, the female figure represents Hatshepsut, depicting her in a crude and demeaning way as being sexually dominated and shamed by a common man.[26] The intended message of this political pornography is to reduce a woman claiming royal and divine power to a sexual object, to put her "in her place" (cf. Tyldesley 1996: 191). Even a woman who wants to be king is just a woman and any man can sexually subdue her. She may construct her public body as masculine and powerful, yet her personal body remains female/feminine, available to be penetrated and subjugated by men. The strategy here is to show the would-be female king as no more than a female sexual object for male domination. It aims thoroughly to demolish any vestige of Hatshepsut's masculinised public body by focusing on her female personal body, which is characterised as powerless, degraded, and submissive.

First Questions from the Past to the Present

Is it a problem when women take on powerful roles that are pre-defined as masculine by cultural and/or religious traditions? Many people of today might say "No". Yet, in the cultural framework of masculine domination, power remains predominantly masculine-gendered. Therefore, no man, striving for power, is forced to construct his public body as feminine. On the contrary, the masculine candidate for power still avoids anything that might feminise his public body and stresses all that makes him more masculine. If power is masculine, belonging to ideal or admired men in a binary gender system, femininity becomes necessarily defined as non-powerful, as weak and helpless. The more feminine – according to the dominant cultural gender definition – a person appears in his/her public body, the more (s)he is incapable of exerting political or sacral power. That is why powerful women of politics, like Margaret Thatcher or Angela Merkel, design their public image in ways that de-emphasise their femininity. Thatcher, famously, was called "the Iron Lady", suggesting strength, and was said to have received voice coaching to lower her voice; both suggest strategic masculinisation.[27]

What if a society would attribute equal value and power to "feminine" and "masculine"? Most probably, this would be a source of freedom and relief, as it would allow human persons to take on roles without conforming to particular stereotypes, relying instead on talent, suitability, and/or qualifications. My father would not have dared to push me in my stroller in public, for fear his masculinity would be questioned or mocked. However, that was the gender-culture of Bavaria in the late 1950s, while nowadays many young fathers see nothing feminine, let alone effeminate, about caring for their children, even babies. Many of them may see it as fatherly responsibility and, therefore, as firmly masculine. This shows that there is scope and hope for change. But what if modern societies would not only attribute the same value to femininity and masculinity but go another step further and de-gender and de-binary tasks and roles in family, business, politics, and all other areas? Would this not be a way to liberate and fully humanise men, women, and persons of all other genders and sexes?

The last words of this chapter must be dedicated to an evaluation of Hatshepsut's historical role. Although such a judgement is not really necessary in an academic context, it is found in so many publications about this ruler that I cannot resist adding my own. Of course, it would be anachronistic to interpret Hatshepsut as a pacifist, feminist or social reformer. Yet, I think she deserves to be honoured as a pioneer in gender formation. In an independent and creative way, she redefined and reconstructed the gendering of her role and the relationship between her personal body and her public one. Although she defined herself by the daughter-relation to her fathers, Thutmose I and Amun, it is also clear that she was the author of her script. She was the one who designed her fathers in exactly the way she needed them. Therefore, her father-concepts fulfil a liberating function – at least concerning the construction of her own biography.

Notes

1 I try to avoid the term "pharaoh" as far as possible, as it is more appropriately applied to later times when *per* ⌷ *a'a* ⇌ ("great house, palace") became a synonym for the king of Egypt. The term was not used for the king prior to the 13th-century BCE and was more often used in Ptolemaic times, not least, because it avoided royal terminology in reference to a "foreign" king (cf. Shaw & Nicholson 2008: 171, 248–249).
2 My spelling follows Shaw and Nicholson (2008: 137).
3 Due to the iconic, i.e. non-narrative, character of Egyptian mythology, the sources rendering narrative texts of the Horus myth are relatively young, although the myth itself is very old. Allusions to it can be found already in the pyramid texts of the Old Kingdom. A canonical version of the tale never existed. English translations of some variations of the legend can be found with Budge (1994: 96–105, 198–248) and Lichtheim (1976: 214–223).
4 When the king passes on, he is transformed into Osiris, father of Horus and eternal king of the otherworld. "By at least the 5th Dynasty (2494–2345 BC) the dead king was identified with Osiris, while the living ruler was equated with his son Horus" (Shaw & Nicholson 2008: 238). This transformation, necessary to ensure the king's eternal life, is also linked with hegemonic masculinity, as it is a process whereby the human king becomes Osiris, the father-god.
5 In most cases, the king's mother, who often is the most powerful woman at court even after the king attains adulthood

A Female King? 29

(cf. Shaw & Nicholson 2008: 267), would be expected to reign in the name of her son if (and as long as) he is a child.

6 Emphasising the combative strength and procreative power of the ruler, the tail was integrated into the royal regalia at a very early stage of Egyptian history. It appears already on the Narmer Palette (ca. 3200–3000 BCE, in the Predynastic Period). This famous masterpiece forms part of the Egyptian Museum's splendid collection in Cairo, identified in the *Journal d'Entrée* as JE32169 and in the *Catalogue Général* as CG14716.

7 Unlike many other Egyptian obelisks, Domitian's one (today at the Piazza Navona) was not taken from an Egyptian site. Instead, it was designed and created, especially for the emperor, by an Egyptian priestly expert. See photos, description, and translation of the hieroglyphic texts in Lembke (1994: 15–17, 37–41, 210–212).

8 The fragment of a relief found at the Karnak temple complex renders Hatshepsut's title ḥmt nswt wrt and depicts her offering liquids, dressed in the garments typical for a Great Royal Wife in the New Kingdom: breast-free pinafore dress, the vulture-hood (relating her to Nekhbet and other maternal goddesses), with double-plumed headgear (relating her to Amun and other celestial gods). See fig. 1 in Kügler (2017: 114). For the history and meaning of the vulture-hood cf. Brunner-Traut (1977).

9 "This system was used, from at least as early as the Middle Kingdom, in order to ensure that the transfer of power took place with the minimum of disruption and instability" (Shaw & Nicholson 2008: 81). Co-regencies are highly probable for Amenemhat I > Senusret I > Amenemhat II > Senusret II. (cf. Schneider 1994: 52–54, 264–267). One may add that the model of the 12th Dynasty might have been of special attractiveness for Hatshepsut, because a female king, Sobekneferu, stood at its end, although with a rather short reign only (cf. Schneider 1994: 175–176).

10 The term "public" does not refer so much to a human audience, which was very small, as only members of the upper class (i.e. the royal administration) could see the royal artefacts. The most relevant audience was gods and goddesses.

11 Famous examples are exhibited at New York (USA) by the Metropolitan Museum and at Leiden (Netherlands) by the Rijksmuseum van Oudheden (cf. Roehrig 2005: 170–172); online material: https://www.metmuseum.org/art/collection/search/544450 (accessed 13/04/2022); https://www.metmuseum.org/art/collection/search/544849 (accessed 13/04/2022); https://commons.wikimedia.org/wiki/Category:Statues_of_Hatshepsut_in_the_Rijksmuseum_van_Oudheden (accessed 13/04/2022).

12 See Naville 1898: plate LVI (a graphic reduced in size is accessible in Kügler 2017: 125).

13 On the New Kingdom's cultural standards for the representation of nudity (cf. Robins 1996).
14 Some examples: *nṯr nfr* is changed to *nṯrt nfrt* ("perfect/visible god" to "perfect/visible goddess"), *nb-t3.wj* to *nbt-t3.wj* ("Lord of the two lands" to "Lady of the two lands") and *s3-R^c [n ẖt=f]* to *s3t-R^c [nt ẖt=f]* ("son of Re [from his body]" to "daughter of Re [from his body]"). My transcription follows Hannig (1997).
15 The hieroglyph ⌐⌐ for *ma'at* is used as the pedestal for the royal throne. Thutmose I's reign is based on *ma'at* and so is that of Hatshepsut, whom he designates his successor.
16 Unfortunately, Brunner's wonderful plates only refer to the relief series in the "birth chamber" of Amenhotep III at Luxor.
17 The texts in scene IV (Brunner 1986: 42–45) give the impression that the father is the unique origin of the child, while the mother just receives and incubates the child in her womb. If that represents the general idea of a child's origin in ancient Egypt, the high importance assigned to breastfeeding would be more than understandable. By giving her milk to the baby, a mother creates relationship and affiliation in addition to transferring her own characteristics to the child. By means of divine wet-nurses suckling the king, he comes to be defined and inaugurated as a member of the divine family.
18 Ahmose, Hatshepsut's mother, was the daughter of King Ahmose I and Great Wife of King Thutmose I. See the family tree at Roehrig (2005: 7).
19 Kügler (2017: 122) offers a nicely reconstructed graphic.
20 On the cultural meaning of breastfeeding, see Kügler (2017: 68–71, for Egypt) and Pedrucci (2019, for other cultures).
21 Probably the tradition that Hathor, whose name translates as "House of Horus", is the mother of Horus is even older than the one, which identifies Isis as Horus' mother (cf. Shaw & Nicholson 2008: 136). As Hathor and Isis were identified or unified with each other, it was easy to switch between Hathor and Isis if necessary.
22 The Egyptian word *nfrw* could also mean "perfectness", "visibility" or "being good", and "(bodily) manifestation (of the divine)" (cf. Hannig (1997: 409).
23 Images of these Osiris-pillars can be found at https://commons.wikimedia.org/wiki/File:Deir_el_Bahari_080410.jpg (accessed 13/04/2022) and https://www.metmuseum.org/art/collection/search/549032 (accessed 13/04/2022).
24 The influence of feminist views on Hatshepsut's reign, seen in many recent publications, does not exclude judgements following the patriarchal view of history. For example, Grimm and Schoske speak of "legitimation opera" (1999: 14: "Legitimationsoper") and of "artificial legitimation" (1999: 33: "Künstliche Legitimation"),

as if they try to insinuate that other kings – due to their male sex? – had a "natural" legitimation and needed no "opera". Are we supposed to believe that these men "really" were the sons of Amun-Ra?

25 For the text of the of this long-serving official's autobiography, see Breasted (1906). The crucial point is that Ahmose Pen-Nekhbet only refers to Hatshepsut as a royal wife, although he mentions her throne-name Maat-Ka-Ra: "The Divine Consort, the Great King's-Wife, Makere (M^ɔ ^{c}·t-k^ɔ-R^c, Hatshepsut), triumphant, repeated honors to me. I reared her eldest daughter, the Royal Daughter, Neferure (Nefrw-R^c), triumphant, while she was a child upon the breast" (English translation by Breasted 1906: 143–144).

26 Even if one would follow Tyldesley's (1996: 190–191) interpretation that the graffito is showing a consensual sexual act between Hatshepsut and her supposed lover Senenmut, the message would not change much as the penetration in itself is seen as an act of masculine domination (see Chapter 3).

27 In her many years as *Bundeskanzlerin*, Chancellor Angela Merkel very seldom was seen at any major political occasion in a skirt or dress. Instead, she reserved the long ball gown – culturally defined as typically feminine – to more private occasions, like her annual visit to the Wagner festival at Bayreuth. For discussion on Merkel's public outfits, see https://www.deutschlandfunknova.de/beitrag/merkel-und-co-der-hosenanzug-als-macher-outfit (accessed 13/04/2022). Merkel, however, never went as far as Maria-Elisabeth Schäffler, one of the richest businesspersons in Germany, and one of the owners of Schaeffler Group AG. She appeared in public business occasions always in perfectly masculine outfits. Cf. https://www.sueddeutsche.de/wirtschaft/schaeffler-mitten-im-umbruch-1.4546103 (accessed 13/04/2022).

2 Hatshepsut Baptised

Christian Women as Sons of God

Ordinary People in the Royal Role of Horus and Osiris

Hatshepsut was not the last woman to masculinise her public body. Although most women – like, indeed, most men – were excluded from political power-making in the monarchic states of the ancient Mediterranean world, we find, hundreds of years after Hatshepsut's reign, many people who strived for the royal roles of Horus and Osiris.

As my Egyptology teacher Ursula Rößler-Köhler (1991) established, Hellenistic-Roman Egypt saw religious patterns originally reserved only for the king, becoming transferred also to ordinary people. This process started already in the late New Kingdom (ca. 1550–1069 BCE)[1] but gained its full momentum in the time of Hellenistic (ca. 300–30 BCE) and Roman (from 30 BCE on) rule over Egypt. Hellenistic kings, like the Roman emperors after them, were, to some extent, integrated into Egypt's mytho-political traditions, but their reign was not seen as fully compliant with or equal to the Egyptian royal role, especially with regard to religious functions and requirements central to the meaning of kingship.[2] The hiatus between religion and politics caused by the experience of ethnically and culturally foreign (i.e. Persian, Macedonian, and then Roman) domination gave space to leave political power to the foreign king while transferring religious (and now depoliticised) roles, formerly held by Egyptian kings, to other authorities. Among

DOI: 10.4324/9781003269977-3

the strategies to cope with this religious deficit brought about by foreign rule, we find non-royal individuals taking on the role of Horus during their lifetime and of Osiris in the otherworld. Identifying spiritually with Horus, son of Isis, was not only a central idea of many mystery cults dedicated to Isis and her son but was also a widespread and well-documented[3] pattern of individual spirituality (cf. Kügler 1997: 123–131), in Egypt as well as in almost every other region of the ancient Mediterranean world. Moreover, the idea of becoming united[4] with Osiris was very popular and is found in many funerary texts of Hellenistic-Roman time (cf. Smith 2017: 356–421). As source texts stem from the funerals of *both* men and women, it is clear that turning into Osiris post-mortem was no longer only a male prerogative.

Something that was extraordinary for Hatshepsut and isolated other women[5] of earlier times was very much more popularised and democratised in Hellenistic-Roman Egypt (and even beyond): women, after their death, were united with Osiris and became part of a male god's extended personality. Thus, their religious body was masculinised while their personal body, at the same time, remained female. The personal body, which was more than the mummified physical remains in the coffin, or the mummy portrait,[6] was secured in a similar way as in Hatshepsut's case: namely, predominantly through written texts. This was perfunctory and straightforward as funerary texts associated with a mummy were usually pre-manufactured, leaving blank only the space for the birth-name of the deceased. These texts were customised by simply adding the name of the deceased.[7] When, in the case of a woman, a feminine name was added, the formula "Osiris (of) NN[8]" implied a gender conflict very similar to that of Hatshepsut. Sometimes, referring to the deceased female with the formula "Hathor (of) NN" tempered this conflict. When the deceased female was transformed into Hathorian form, the post-mortem gender was in harmony with the gender of the personal body during its lifetime. Mark Smith (2017), however, rightly points out that using "the locution 'Hathor of NN' did not mean that women ceased to be designated as 'Osiris of NN'. Like men, they could still be called this until belief in the Osirian afterlife came to an end" (2017: 417).

Although we can almost be sure that the Apostle Paul did not know any details of Egyptian mortuary theology and funerary practice, we find a religious pattern in his baptismal teaching that is strikingly similar to the deceased's intention of being transfigured into the Osirian form so popular in Egyptian (and Egyptianising) Osiris religion. Especially, the gender conflict Paul's teaching implies is analogous to that between the personal body of an Egyptian woman and her eternal Osirian body.

Baptism Effects "being in Christ"

Although Paul's letters do not provide us with any systematic theory of baptism, we can learn about his understanding of this initiation rite of becoming Christian from some few texts, chiefly Romans 6 and Galatians 3. As Galatians 3:26–28 deals explicitly with gender topics, it is the more interesting text for our purposes; although we will look at Romans 6 also. The Greek text and my almost verbatim translation read as follows:

> [26] Πάντες γὰρ υἱοὶ θεοῦ ἐστε διὰ τῆς πίστεως ἐν Χριστῷ Ἰησοῦ·
> [26] For you are all sons of God through your faith in Jesus Christ:
> [27] ὅσοι γὰρ εἰς Χριστὸν ἐβαπτίσθητε,
> [27] for whosoever you were baptised in Christ,
> Χριστὸν ἐνεδύσασθε.
> You put on Christ;
> [28] οὐκ ἔνι Ἰουδαῖος οὐδὲ Ἕλλην,
> [28] There is neither Jew nor Hellene,
> οὐκ ἔνι δοῦλος οὐδὲ ἐλεύθερος,
> There is not slave and freeperson,
> οὐκ ἔνι ἄρσεν καὶ θῆλυ·
> There is not male and female;
> πάντες γὰρ ὑμεῖς εἷς ἐστε ἐν Χριστῷ Ἰησοῦ.
> for you are all one in Christ Jesus.[9]

As is widely accepted among scholars, Paul in this passage adapts an ancient credo, which was likely spoken or sung in conjunction with the baptismal liturgy (cf. Schnelle 2003: 316–318).

Although the precise differentiation between the pre-Pauline credo and the Pauline frame text remains disputed, the core of the tradition is distilled in the statement:

> You put on Christ;
> There is neither Jew nor Hellene,
> There is not slave and free,
> There is not male and female.[10]

This baptismal text most probably derives from the early Christian congregation at the Syrian (nowadays Turkish) city of Antiochia, which was important for the Christian formation of Paul after his conversion.[11]

I am assuming that new members put off their clothes (which symbolise their former, pagan identity) before entering the water more or less naked. When leaving the water, they put on new, most probably white, clothing, symbolising their new identity "in Christ". So, one may think that the congregation recited the baptismal text, quoted in Galatians 3:27–28, to explain solemnly to the newly baptised Christians what had happened to them by the water of baptism. In this ritual context, the central message of the hymn consists in relating the new dress of the freshly baptised to their new status as a representation or personification of the Messiah. The baptismal creed annihilates the basic status differences of antique society and associates this annihilation with the baptism, which is interpreted as "putting on Christ".

Within the terms of cultural symbolism of clothing, common in ancient societies, such putting on is not merely an external gesture. Rather, clothing expresses the role and the status of a person in society. It is, in a sense, an integral part of the person, shaping their public body. As the antique notion of personhood focuses on the role of the individual in society, that is to say, on the individual's status and impact, the clothing as a part of the public body was of considerable importance.

To give an example, for the High Priest at the Jewish temple in Jerusalem, the priestly garment is of such importance that he is not even able to perform the duties of his office without it (cf. MacDonald 2019).[12] Therefore, the Roman occupiers (following King Herod's example) only needed to lock it away if they wanted to keep the High Priest from exercising his office independently (cf. Schäfer 2010: 113 f). The clothing of the king, too, is integral to his role; it manifests and makes visible his royal majesty. When a king wears golden or silver clothing, he sometimes asserts that he is representing divine qualities in his royal office. Emperor Nero, for example, "dressed in purple robes and a Greek coat embroidered with golden stars" (Suetonius, Nero 25,1) to signify and display his position as divine ruler with cosmic power. For Jewish kings, however, it would be precarious, even blasphemous, to claim divine royalty. As Jewish historian Josephus recounts, God punishes King Agrippa I with death because the latter does not reject the flatteries offered to him by his entourage. They called him God when he wore silver robes in public, signalling claims to divine dignity (Jos. Ant. 19,8,1).[13] The immense importance of clothing can, moreover, be found in the Jesus-tradition, for example in the miracle story of the healing of the bleeding woman. When this woman in need secretly touches Jesus's clothing, she is not only healed right away but Jesus also *feels* powerful energy flowing from it (Mk 5:27–30).[14] When, in this popular conception of magical transmission such power is attributed to Jesus's clothing, one can begin to imagine what it means to dress with the Messiah himself.

Whoever wears Christ as her or his clothing is transfigured into Christ in terms of status, role, and function. Being dressed with the Messiah means transforming one's public body into that of Christ and, thus, participating in his divine dignity and power. The message of the traditional baptismal text, therefore, can be seen as signifying the results of conversion. Even if the relation between God the Father and Christ the Son is not mentioned in the short text, it seems that Christian believers' redemption means no less than sharing in the divine status of Jesus, the messianic son of God.

Paul holds this view, too, and makes it even more explicit. In his introduction to the credo he emphasises that all believers are "sons of God in Christ" (Gal 3:26). It is not a coincidence that Paul does not use the gender-neutral term "children of God" here. For one, the Messiah is a male figure and all who put him on are consequently *sons* of God "in Christ". Secondly, a son had a completely different status in ancient society than a daughter.

Only a son was considered the representation or replication of the father; usually, only a son had the right to inherit property;

and only he (as deputy of the father) had oversight of his sisters. As Carola Reinsberg (1989) points out, in most Greek city states, a daughter had no fortune and was not entitled to inherit property. If a daughter was not yet married when her father died, she was part of the estate and was passed on to the closest male relative as part of the inheritance. A woman was not an autonomous person in legal affairs. She could therefore not engage in business transactions, could not testify as a witness in court, or start legal proceedings of her own. All of her life, she was *de facto* subjected to the power of a lord (κύριος). Her lord was the father, the husband, or some other male relative (cf. Reinsberg 1989: 36–37; Neils 2011: 58–66). In Hellenistic times, sociocultural changes[15] eased these constraints considerably. "A new phenomenon appeared in this period, namely the political and public prominence of specific elite women, who exercised power in a number of ways and left behind a range of evidence about themselves. These women need not have been be royal [...], and they perceived themselves as having a right to take an active role in the lives, politics, and even wars of their cities [...]. Female public patronage began in this period, on many levels, from helping individual citizens to paying public debts to providing important public buildings. This pattern of female prominence and participation in public life appeared throughout this cosmopolitan period" (James & Dillon 2012: 229).

In Hellenistic-Roman time, there were indeed female philosophers, female public benefactors, entrepreneurs, authors, and ship owners (cf. Thraede 1972: 223), but these women remained the exception confirming the rule.[16] The general perception of women as inferior beings was never overcome.

In the cultural context of masculine domination, it would not have profited Christian women to be called "daughters of God". As daughters, they would have been subordinate to their "brothers" in the congregation and only indirectly would they have shared in the divine character of their heavenly "father". By declaring all believers *sons* of God, however, Paul attributes the same status to all members of the congregation – to women as well as to men. Hence, he concludes his citation of the Antiochian baptismal text with "you are all one" (εἷς). By using the *masculine* singular instead of the *neuter* singular (ἕν),

Paul expresses that the unity of Christians is not an abstract one; it is a body. As all Christians, including female believers, are "in Christ", i.e. in the messianic *son* of God, their unity is that of a masculine, messianic body. Being the living "body" of the Messiah (cf. 1 Cor 12:27), the Christian congregation unites all members into a *masculine* unity and not into a neuter or ungendered one. Thus, the collective body of the Church and the public/religious body of each single member are masculine bodies.

For modern readers, this soteriological "trans-gendering" may appear as strange as that of Hatshepsut. However, within the remit of the cultural conditions of masculine domination, Paul's baptismal teaching is an attempt to do something new. The soteriological masculinisation of women's religious bodies is not about perpetuating misogynistic ideology, but about achieving gender equality in a misogynistic context. Paul tries to create a space of generalised masculinity, hoping that if *all* the members of a group are defined as men, the gender of hierarchy vanishes and, in a way, the inner space of the group becomes "gender-neutral" in as far as there is no longer any gender difference.[17] If all Christians are "sons of God" in their public Church body, the personal body and gender of any Christian becomes less relevant. Even if the personal body is female, the person can have access to all roles in the messianic body of the Church, even to those that are traditionally defined as masculine. That is why Paul supports a gender-neutral Church practice that allows any person to take on any role in the congregation without regard for social status, ethnic-religious origin, and gender.[18]

Gender neutrality already belonged to the central claims of the Antiochian creed that Paul uses in Galatians 3. Interestingly, when the category of gender is at stake, the terms "male" (ἄρσεν) and "female" (θῆλυ) are employed (Gal 3:28). This suggests that already the Syrian tradition was concerned with eliminating the contours and centrality of the personal body. As the Church is seen as the space for a new reality "in Christ", differences defined by the old world of sin (slave vs. slaveholder, Jew vs. pagan, male vs. female) have no relevance within the Church. For this reason, early Christian congregations have female deacons, like Phoebe (Rom 16:1), female apostles, like Junia (Rom 16:7), female hosts (cf. Pilhava 2017).

This emerges clearly from Paul's epistles, particularly the letter to the Christians in Rome. Furthermore, the Roman community illustrates that the early Christian ecclesiology of generalised gender was not limited to the congregations under Antiochian-Pauline influence. The Roman congregation arose independently of Paul, and a team of women played a prominent role in it.[19]

It is, of course, tempting to compare the masculinisation of Christian women's public bodies with the masculinisation of Hatshepsut as king and with later Egyptian women's transfiguration into Osirian form. Not only the process itself is similar but the consequences, too, are comparable. In all these cases the masculinisation of a woman's public body results in granting access to roles and statuses that otherwise were reserved for men: be it kingship, Osirian eternity, or a new existence "in Christ". Of course, one should not exaggerate or overstate the similarities. Christian women became king only in a spiritual way, not in a political one. Furthermore, the masculinisation of their public bodies pertained to a status that can be experienced here and now, while the Osirian body of Egyptian women came into being post-mortem. And yet, this difference should not be seen as too profound, given that Paul's theology understands the life of Christians as life after death in a specific way. In Romans 6:2–3 Paul states that Christians lose their previous life through conversion. The believers are said, to die with Christ in baptism. Therefore, they are dead for the non-believing, sinful world. Moreover, because sharing in Jesus's death also means sharing in his resurrection, Christians live a new life, which is eternal and symbolically post-mortem. Thus, it can be compared with the Osirian existence on the level of the religious body. The important difference is with the personal body, which is mummified in the Egyptian case and alive in the Christian case.

Should All "Sons of God" Look Like Men?

The new body of Christians is a reality "in Christ" and shows its effects primarily within the Church, which is the "body of Christ". When a Christian woman left a meeting of the congregation, she definitely occupied her personal body. If she also inhabited alongside this her masculinised Church-body is an open question. Maybe, she left her religious body and returned to her female public body, whenever she returned to her profane life in the "old world". We do not know of any Christian woman who tried to adapt her public body of everyday life to her religious body or Church masculinity. Claiming a masculine public body in extra-Church society and striving for functions and roles determined masculine, could, conceivably and plausibly, have constituted a gender revolution initiated by Christian belief. Unfortunately, our sources do not tell us anything about such a revolution.

We do know, however, of some Christian women who assimilated their personal body to their Church body. Paul is arguing with these women in 1 Corinthians 11:2–16.[20] Unfortunately, Paul does not clearly describe the problem in detail, as his Corinthian addressees knew it well. Yet, we can reconstruct it when looking to the gender oppositions he uses:

Man (praying and prophesying)	Woman (praying and prophesying)
Having something "down from his head"/ κατὰ κεφαλῆς ἔχων means shame (11:4)	Having the head "uncovered"/ ἀκατακαλύπτῳ τῇ κεφαλῇ is equivalent to shorn or shaved and means shame (11:5 f)
Should not "cover his head"/ κατακαλύπτεσθαι τὴν κεφαλὴν (11:7)	Should not pray „uncovered "/ ἀκατακάλυπτον (11:13)
To "have long hair"/ κομᾷ is a shame (11:14)	To "have long hair"/ κομᾷ is an honour as the "long hair"/ ἡ κόμη is given her "as a cover"/ ἀντὶ περιβολαίου (11:15)
Result Inadequate for a man: covered head = something down form the head = long hair Adequate for a man: short hair = uncovered head	Inadequate for a woman: uncovered = shorn/shaved = uncovered Adequate for a woman: long hair = covered head

As the table shows, Paul tries to define how the head of a praying or prophesying Christian should look like according to gender order. The man should have his head not covered with long hair and the woman should have her head covered with long hair. The "problem" that he is confronting here most probably arose when a group of Christian women tried to harmonise their personal body with the masculinity of their religious body by cutting their hair short. In Hellenistic-Roman time, short hair was defined as typically, even "naturally", masculine (1 Cor 11:14), while long hair was seen as "natural" for women (1 Cor 11:15). Thus, short hair was an easy way for Christian women to masculinise their personal body. Given the absence of plastic surgery, it was possibly even the *only* way of assimilating the female and feminine personal body to the masculine Church body. The religious motivation for this masculinisation can be seen in the gender message of Paul's baptismal theology, as discussed already.

As can be gleaned from 1 Corinthians 12, the early Christian baptismal text, quoted in Galatians 3, was part of Paul's baptismal preaching in Corinth also. He writes:

καὶ γὰρ ἐν ἑνὶ πνεύματι ἡμεῖς πάντες εἰς ἓν σῶμα ἐβαπτίσθημεν,
For in *one* Spirit we all into *one* body were baptised
εἴτε Ἰουδαῖοι εἴτε Ἕλληνες εἴτε δοῦλοι εἴτε ἐλεύθεροι,
– whether Jews or Greek, whether slaves or free;
καὶ πάντες ἓν πνεῦμα ἐποτίσθημεν.
and all we were given the one Spirit to drink.
(1 Cor 12:13)

However, he alludes to the Antiochian tradition in 1 Corinthians 12 without repeating the statement regarding gender. This is not surprising if the conflict about crew cuts arose from those very statements. It also means that we have to assume that Paul brought this text to Corinth, along with the idea that the congregation should have a gender-neutral structure. This interpretation is supported by the fact that Paul in 1 Corinthians 11 never denies women's right to play an active role in the congregation. He never questions that women are entitled to pray and prophesy in the same manner as men (11:4–5).[21] He "only" wants them not to look like men when they do so.[22]

If we imagine the young Christian congregation in Corinth hearing the message that all believers are *sons of God*, that all are *one* in the masculine body of Christ, in the cultural context of masculine domination, it seems very plausible that women might understand the teaching that there is *not male and not female* as a programme of general masculinisation. This, in turn, would make sense of the declaration that personal gender is irrelevant, as well as of the masculinisation of Christian women's personal bodies.[23] Both are implied in Paul's letter addressing women's conduct at Corinth.

Paul and the Gender Politics of Today's Churches

The Antiochian baptismal text, which Paul cites in Galatians 3, is dogmatically speaking a high-ranking text. It proclaims the de-gendering of roles and functions within the Church and connects this to the practice of baptism (i.e. the essence of Christian existence as "being in Christ"). This renders obsolete the idea of a "God-willed" subordination of women to men. Yet, globally speaking, the majority of Christians are not following this apostolic teaching. Instead, many churches – among them the Roman Catholic Church[24] – focus on gender discriminatory aspects of Paul's argumentation and on its deutero-Pauline intensification (e.g. in 1 Tim 2:11–15 and Eph 5:22–33). Even Pope Francis, often seen as a reform-oriented church leader, does nothing to change the rule that women in view of their sex cannot function as priestly representations of Christ. This most probably owes to the fact that he grants the doctrinal authority of a binding tradition to this custom. However, taking the pre-Pauline teaching into account, I must conclude that this practice is a sinful error, which has led the Church away from the apostolic gospel.[25] Although since the 1970s many denominations have decided to remove gender restrictions related with ordination,[26] one has to realise that – under the aspects of membership – the big churches like the Roman Catholic Church and the Orthodox Churches did not change in this point. This error cannot be justified by the separation of the grace of baptism from the grace of ordination, often found in official Catholic documents. This argument is a theological method of excluding women from ordination while at the same time ascribing equal dignity to all baptised Christians regardless of their sex.[27] The argument is an attempt to solve gender conflicts by a kind of "gender apartheid": men and women have different roles and functions in the church but these different spaces do not imply any hierarchy in worth or honour. What is typically masculine is not of higher value than what is typically feminine. That this is not more than a rhetorical strategy to defend the patriarchal *status quo* can be learned from the fact that there is nothing in the church that is exclusively reserved for women. All the activities that are declared as typically feminine (e.g. imitating Mother Mary) can be exerted by men as well, while on the other side the activities and roles that are declared as typically masculine (like ordination) are reserved for men and cannot be accessed by women. That is exactly what gender injustice is about.

Furthermore, the separation of baptism and ordination misses the fundamental character of baptismal grace, which precedes and defines every structural formation of the Church. Such a separation either denies the effect of salvation and baptism or it separates ordination from salvation and alleges an additional, independent appointment by Jesus. As is well known, there is no historical proof for the latter as Jesus was not interested in founding a church but in presenting a vision of what it meant to be Israel.[28]

Of course, one could take the position that doing away with ordination altogether would be one way of achieving gender equity within the Church, but as long as it exists one should keep questioning the gender bias in the Roman Catholic Church as well as in other churches. Paul and the pre-Pauline tradition, at any rate, regard baptism and salvation as the fundamental transformation of all Christians, one that necessarily leads to a gender-undifferentiated Church structure. Since all who have been baptised are "sons of God", all Christians are equal in all aspects of Church life. Anyone who claims that one half of the Church is unable sacramentally to represent Christ because of their sex, must be told – in keeping with the apostolic tradition – that (s)he *de facto* denies salvation and takes biology to be more important than what occurs through faith and baptism. This amounts to nothing less than the radical annihilation of the Christian message of salvation. If gender-undifferentiated salvation does not bring about so much as an effect on office structures within the Church, how could it ever bring about salvific effects in the world at large? The worldly effects, however, are a crucial criterion for the truth of Christian belief which from its origins was defined as a "truth to be *done*" (Joh 3:21; 1 Joh 1:6). The most urgent problem is not the inner church question if some women can be ordained or not. That is an internal question of church life relevant, let us say, for less than one Christian per ten thousand church members. What is much more relevant is the message sent out by reserving ordination to men only. It says to all the Christians and to the rest of the world that men have the right and the power to exclude women from central areas of dignity and power and that this exclusion is executing God's will. This fatal message declares gender justice as not only necessary but even ungodly. Therefore, one can say that church has to change not only to solve inner problems. It is for the sake of human development that Christianity must come back to the role of an advocate of gender equality and gender fairness – a role played by early Christians as the gender avant-garde of their time.

Notes

1 A short overview over this important era can be found at Shaw and Nicholson (2008: 225).
2 The most important difference between Hellenistic kings and the Roman emperor was their presence within the country. While the Roman Caesars (ruling over Egypt since Augustus defeated Cleopatra and Marc Antony in 31/30 BCE) were absent with only a *Praefectus* representing them, the kings of the Ptolemaic dynasty (following Alexander's conquest in 332 BCE) were residing at Egypt. Despite their presence and their high efforts to fulfil their religious duties (e.g. by generously funding the building of new temples), there was, however, always a religio-political problem with their rule. As the traditional role of the Egyptian king included "defeating the enemies of the gods" (among them all foreigners threatening Egypt), the Ptolemaic dynasty, stemming

from Macedonian Greece, was in the uncomfortable situation of fighting themselves – at least in a symbolic way. The problem can be seen clearly at the Horus temple of Edfu, where Ptolemaios XII is depicted in the traditional pose of "smiting the enemies" in front of Horus (cf. the photo at Shaw & Nicholson 2008: 101), while the inscriptions list "the Greek" (i.e. the ethnic group of the king) among these enemies. As the Hellenistic-Roman rulers regarded their culture as superior to the "old-fashioned" culture of Egypt, neither the Hellenistic nor the Roman rulers agreed in giving up their ethno-cultural identity. Thus, the conflict persisted until Egypt was christianised (cf. Bowman 1986, Casagrande-Kim 2014, and Bagnall 2021).

3 A statistical analysis of museum collections at Cairo and Paris shows that 43% of the religious terracotta objects are dedicated to Harpocrates ("Horus-the-child") and 18% Isis. So, Horus and Isis together cover more than half of all sacral objects, while the many other deities of the ancient Egyptian pantheon share in the rest (cf. Kügler 1997: 130, incl. note 190). Additionally, religious amulets, indicating the user's spiritual relationship with a deity, often show Isis or Horus, or both. See e.g. the wonderful piece at the British Museum: https://www.britishmuseum.org/collection/object/Y_EA11638 (accessed 13/04/2022).

4 Smith states, "[the locution Osiris (of) NN] does not identify the deceased with Osiris. Rather it associates them with that god in a particular type of relationship where the deity looks after them and provides their needs" (2017: 373). Becoming "one" with Osiris, therefore, has to be understood in a way that the deceased is transfigured into an Osirian form that unites her/him with Osiris without losing her/his own identity.

5 Smith (2017: 389) mentions a woman from the time of the Old Kingdom as the first example to bear the title "Osiris of NN".

6 On the cultural and theological importance of the Egyptian mummy portraits, cf. Borg (1998).

7 Inserting the name of the deceased sometimes was done very carelessly. See the example of a papyrus translated by Sternberg-el-Hotabi (1988). She states that in the second half of the text the spaces reserved for the name of the deceased were simply left blank without inserting the name (1988: 405). Apparently, mentioning the name at the beginning of the text was seen as sufficient to secure the individual presence of the deceased who was to be transformed into Osirian form.

8 "NN" here substitutes the individual name of the deceased.

9 All translations of biblical texts and ancient authors are mine unless other information is given.

10 I take my bearings from Bormann (2008: 110).

11 According to New Testament information, Paul assisted Barnabas in his apostolic mission for the church of Antiochia (cf. Acts 11:20–26; Gal 2:11).
12 On the gender significance of clothing, see McKay (2017).
13 The story, which appears in different form in Acts 12:21–23, simultaneously demonstrates how difficult it was for Jewish kings to escape the dominant ideology of the ruler's divinity.
14 Cf. also the healing power of the tassels of Jesus's clothes (Mt 14:36).
15 These changes have, of course, several reasons. One of them is the loss of importance that the Greek city states experienced. The bigger political unities of post-Alexander monarchies together with the economic, cultural, and linguistic "globalisation" in the Mediterranean world led to a higher mobility of people and weakened the structures of patriarchal households.
16 On working women in general, cf. Neils (2011: 92–121); on the role of women on Greek islands, cf. Stavrianopoulou (2006), on Jewish women in Minor Asia, cf. Trebilco (1991: 104–126); for Hellenistic Egypt, see Melaerts (2002); on the special situation of royal women in the Seleuci dynasty, cf. Coşkun (2016); on daughters in Roman elite families, cf. Hallett (1984).
17 This is still a de-gendered space that is built from the material of masculine supremacy, as gender-irrelevance is achieved by general masculinising – not by feminising all members. Paul's concept obviously carries the implication that for females to be masculinised is a step up, whereas for men to be feminised signifies downward social movement. The default assumption that the highest form of a human being is a male one is not overcome.
18 Of course, the image of Paul's gender policy changes drastically, if one sees the order that women should be silent at church (1 Cor 14:33b–36) as coming directly from Paul. That is, however, highly improbable as Paul even in 1 Cor 11:2–16 never questions that women are entitled to speak in the assembly in the same manner as men (11:4–5). Cf. the short summary of all of the arguments given by Gielen (2017: 12 f.). She concludes, "The passage is a post-Pauline insertion, which was made under the influence of the Pastoral letters" (2017: 13 [my translation]).
19 Paul mentions Mary (Rom 16:6), Tryphaina, Tryphosa, and Persis (Rom 16:12) by name. Schreiber (2000) argues that the expression κοπιάω ἐν κυρίῳ / working hard in the Lord (Rom 16:12) is a technical term which Paul uses for "leading the congregation". Meanwhile, Scherer (2016) criticised this claim. In her contribution, she emphasises that Paul's statement does not inform about the concrete position held by the women in question. However, she also states that gender was not a relevant criterion for access

to the roles, duties, and positions within Roman congregations. Thus, in Paul's time, the Roman congregation definitely was part of the broad stream of early Christian non-gendered ecclesiology.

20 Cf. Kügler (2019: 241–242), where I substantiate my understanding of the problem Paul is dealing with in 1 Cor 11:2–16.

21 For this reason (among others), 1 Cor 14:33b–36 cannot come directly from Paul (cf. Gielen 2017: 12 f.).

22 Paul's theological arguments in 1 Cor 11:2–16 partly contradict his own soteriological teaching (cf. Kügler [2019: 253–256] on the theological problem of this contradiction).

23 If Christian women, additionally, were influenced by Platonist concepts (cf. Kügler 2019: 248–251), they could have considered their personal body as doubly inferior – being a *body* and being *female*! What response could be more plausible than to assimilate such an inferior female body to the higher states of masculinity and spirituality? Creating a kind of man-like physical appearance seems a response of high plausibility – at least under the conditions of a cultural system of masculine domination. And, a short haircut appears a quite moderate body modification that could even be hidden when leaving the Christian assembly. Due to the positive bias towards masculinity, it was not necessary that men manipulated their personal body, already conceived as male/masculine. However, Christian men, too, understood their being "in Christ" as a masculinisation. This can be gleaned from the debate about sexual ethics in 1 Corinthians. The Corinthian slogan "It is good for a man (= human being, Greek: ἀνθρώπῳ!) not to touch a woman", which is quoted by Paul (1 Cor 7:1), without rendering his own opinion (cf. Merklein 1983 vs. Leutzsch 2004: 603 f.), reveals, on the one hand, that being male was equated with being fully human and, on the other hand, that Christian men, too, considered it a Christian ideal to pursue full masculinity by overcoming the corporeal-sensual aspects of human life. Popular Platonism understood the domination of sexual desire (conceived of as feminine) as a manifestation of ultimate masculinity. If the *nous*, the intellectual (= masculine) part of the human mind is ruling like a king over the inner life, controlling everything like a sovereign, the person is fully masculine, "a real man" according to popular philosophy of Paul's time.

24 The Roman Catholic Church alone counts more than 1.3 billion. The CIA factbook estimates that 31.1% of the world population were Christians: https://www.cia.gov/the-world-factbook/countries/world/ (accessed 11/01/2022). Based on that information one could estimate that more than the half of the ca. 2.2 billion Christians would be Roman Catholics.

25 A short overview of how the Church fathers argued for the exclusion of women from ordination is given by Dassmann (1997).
26 Unfortunately, there is no precise list of the churches that grant ordination of women (since the 20th century or earlier). However, a short overview can be found at https://en.wikipedia.org/wiki/Ordination_of_women#Christianity (accessed 13/04/2022).
27 Francis adopted this argumentative strategy from Pope John Paul II. For a criticism of the respective statements, see Merklein (1997) (cf. Pope Francis 2013). (cf. also the recent critique of Lüke [2018], who rightly argues that firstly the biological sex is not as stable as papal teaching supposes and secondly the priestly representation refers to Jesus's humanity and not to his masculinity).
28 Meier (2001: 19–288) sees the followers of Jesus structured in concentric circles of different character, none of them defined as priestly. In the New Testament, we do not even find a connection between sacraments and church office (cf. Gielen & Kügler 2014: 97–99).

3 Why One Must Not Turn a Man into a Woman (Egypt – Greece – Rome)

When we talk of rape culture, we often think of sexual violence perpetrated by men against women. Although this is indeed the common pattern in very many cases, one should not forget children and men as victims of sexual violence (cf. Greenough 2021). As we shall see in this chapter, rape culture in ancient times did not put much weight on the sex of the victim. More important is the question of gender, which is related directly with roles in sexual intercourse. The one penetrating is masculine and the penetrated one is feminine. Seen within a framework of masculine domination, feminisation signifies degradation, loss of power, and honour. The question is, however, how the public and personal body are related in the exercise of masculine domination through rape when the victim is male and the perpetrator is not "homosexual" in the modern understanding of gay orientation, identity, and lifestyle.

Two Egyptian Gods Contending for Kingship

The oldest source that I will analyse here in order to understand the relation between public and personal body in cases of violent sexual intercourse between men stems again from Egypt. It is one of the many variations of the Horus myth. As already mentioned, the myth did not know a single canonical form. The variation I want to explore is from a text written in hieratic script on papyrus and from the time of Ramesses V (ca. 1140 BCE). It is now part of the collection in the Chester Beatty Library in Dublin.

The main plot of this text concerns the contest of two gods, Horus and Seth, battling over the succession of Osiris to become king of Egypt.[1] Fighting for power uses sexual means also. One episode tells how Seth tries to penetrate the sleeping Horus. He wants to "make him a woman" in order to render him unable to rule as king. Cunning Horus succeeds in preventing Seth's attack. Using his hand to avoid penetration, he manages secretly to collect Seth's sperm. With the help of his powerful mother Isis, the great magician of the Egyptian pantheon, he gets rid of Seth's sperm by disposing of it in the sewer system. Horus then masturbates to produce his own sperm, which his mother Isis spreads on Seth's favourite vegetables in the garden. On eating his beloved snack, Seth ingests the sperm of Horus and becomes impregnated. When Seth calls the Ennead, the divine High Court, to acknowledge him as legitimate king, he prides himself on having feminised his competitor. As Seth says to the gods: "Let the office of ruler be given to me, for as regards Horus who stands here, I have done a man's deed to him" (Lichtheim 1976: 220). The reaction of the gods shows just how atrocious such a man-to-man penetration was held to be: "Then the Ennead cried out aloud, and they spat out before Horus" (Lichtheim 1976: 220). Their spitting out before the victim is not simply what we would call "victim blaming" today. Rather, it indicates that such violence is not so much a matter of sexual ethics, which would make it necessary to rebuke and punish the rapist (here, Seth) for violating the sexual integrity of another person (here, Horus). Instead, the whole affair is seen exclusively from the perspective of masculine domination: Seth, the rapist, has manifested his masculine power, which is, in the context of a competition for power, appropriate. On the other hand, the penetrated party exemplifies "unmanly" weakness through not being able to defend himself. Thus, shameful femininity is attributed to the victim. As a (supposedly) feminised man, Horus, according to this logic, deserves public contempt. Fortunately for him, Horus has not been penetrated and can laugh at the hysterical reaction of the gods. He tells the Ennead to call for the semen of Seth – and it answers from the sewage system. Then the semen of Horus is called, and it answers from within Seth. Realising that it is Horus, who has played the dominant masculine role by impregnating Seth with his divine sperm, the judges change their mind and acknowledge Horus's claim: "Horus is right, Seth is wrong" (Lichtheim 1976: 220).

The relationship between sexuality and power is extremely tight in this mythical tale. Although gender is not the predominant preoccupation of this text discussing the legitimacy of Horus's succession to his father's throne,[2] the story presupposes a specific idea of how gender and power are linked. This may not reflect the attitude of the author, but it is certainly of cultural and ideological relevance. Ideas of gender and power become clearer when we ask what rape has to do with the ability to be king. If we see the task of a ruler as contributing to the welfare of the population by solving problems and maintaining a peaceful equilibrium, then there is no place for a sexually violent ruler, of course. If, however, the basis for ruling is the establishment of domination by any means, violence, including sexual violence, makes sense. And indeed, Egyptian kingship is linked with brutal violence from its beginning. The already mentioned Narmer Palette[3] (ca. 3200–3000 BCE, Predynastic Period) shows the king with his victims, slaughtered enemies laid in nice rows with their cut-off heads between their legs. Not that Egyptian kings did not solve problems (like raising the fertility of the land with sophisticated networks of canalisation, for instance), but such was not the source or basis of their legitimation. The basic idea of kingship was to fight the permanent threat of chaos by defeating enemies, who were the agents of chaos (Egyptian *isfet*). The king and the other gods, meanwhile, were the forces of order and stability (*ma'at*). The king is a god who can do anything to you, if he only wants to – from taking your property, your health, sexual integrity, or life. However, if you perform perfect subordination, he will show his grace and be the source of your wealth, welfare, and life. Therefore, it is part of the royal majesty that people fear kings. The famous Egyptian novel of Sinuhe is a literary document for the breathtaking fear that the god-king arouses even

52 Why One Must Not Turn a Man into a Woman

when benign (cf. Kügler 2013: 187). Sinuhe, a high-ranking court official returning from exile, says:

> I found his majesty [i.e. Senusret I] on the great throne in a kiosk of gold. Stretched out on my belly, I did not know myself before him, while this god [i.e. the king] greeted me pleasantly. I was like a man seized by darkness. My *ba* [i.e. a kind of soul] was gone, my limbs trembled; my heart was not in my body, I did not know life from death.[4]

Even if *ma'at*, the concept of divine-royal world order is depicted as a beautiful young goddess with a feather on her head, one should not forget that the order she incorporates, must be established again and again through violent subjugation and even killing of enemies. From earliest times on, the royal-divine fight against chaotic forces representing *isfet* includes – at least symbolically – the aspect of violent sexuality. A royal memorial palette (Figure 3.1), more than 5000 years old, displays this quite explicitly: the king in his divine[5] form as bull stands over and defeats a prostrate enemy in human form.

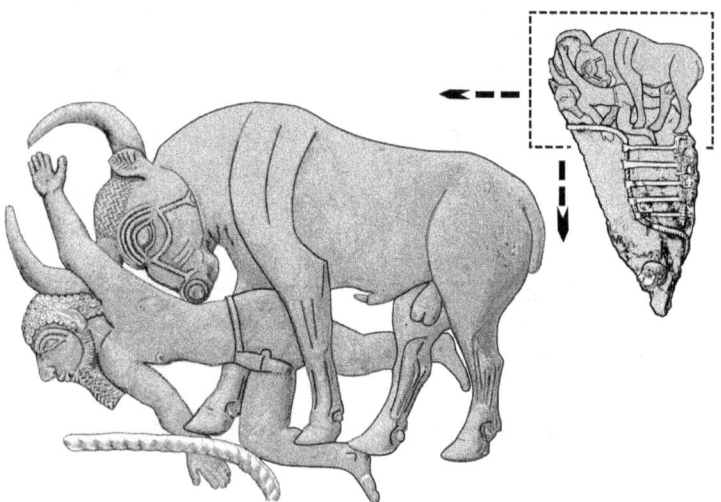

Figure 3.1 The "bull palette"[6]

The defeated man is face down, his back and buttocks facing upwards, while the royal bull is visibly aroused, straddling the man between his front legs, insinuating that he will use not only his horns but also his phallus to subdue and humiliate the enemy. Sex associated with establishing order by defeating chaos has little, even nothing, to do with attraction, lust, or procreation. Instead, the act (or intention) of penetration is a visible manifestation of dominance and power. Because in the typical binary scheme penetrating is masculine and, conversely, being penetrated is feminine, power is clearly gendered as masculine, and the penetration of a man in any exercise of or struggle for power is feminising and debasing. A penetrated man is unmanned and unfit to rule.

Neither the bull palette nor the text on Horus and Seth indicates what belongs to masculinity in addition to being capable of penetrating. Yet it is clear that the sexual act of penetration is understood as an act of domination in a general sense. A man displaying his ability to dominate others sexually proves his ability to dominate others generally. Domination generally is understood in Seth's words, "man's deed" and penetration is a sacrament[7] of masculine domination, all the more so if those penetrated do not consent. Rape, therefore, is an effective way to signify definitive masculine domination. The man capable of exerting his will in spite of the will or consent of others is the ideal masculine ruler.[8] This is a chilling characterisation of ruling, perfectly befitting non-democratic, dictatorial, or monarchic states. Of course, it is also a chilling characterisation of sexuality, lacking any aspect of consent, love, and tenderness. Violent sexuality as a sacrament of masculine domination has only to do with power, strength and subjugation.

It is, however, necessary not to overlook the difference between the personal and the political body. While the rapist displays his masculine public body in harmony with his male personal body, for the raped man, being penetrated means that the public body is unmoored from the personal body. While the personal body's masculinity remains unchanged,[9] the public body is feminised through subjugation. In a cultural code defining domination as masculine and being dominated as feminine, the king as divine autocrat is the "manliest man" in his empire.

The difference between public and personal body, which I use here, may be helpful in understanding ancient cultures, but we have to keep in mind that it is a modern, analytical category that our sources do not overtly describe themselves. This is not least, because acknowledging this difference would weaken the cultural system of masculine domination. The code of this cultural construction – like other cultural codes – succeeds by constructing a human-made system as something natural or divinely ordained. Therefore, any difference between the two bodies is usually ignored or suppressed. We can see this in the mythical tale of the power struggle of Horus and Seth, especially in Seth's pregnancy – a detail somewhat amusing to modern readers. Seeing as we cannot suppose that ancient Egyptians thought that eating sperm would make pregnant, or that men can become pregnant at all, any more than we do, we should realise that these fanciful details follow a strategy of naturalisation. The text ignores biological facts and extends the effect of the public body being raped also to the personal body. The rape of the personal body effects the feminisation of the public body. And *vice versa* the feminisation of the public body reflects on the personal body – by producing pregnancy. Thus, the personal and public body are made indistinguishable in order to naturalise the cultural concept of femininity as being "naturally" subject to masculine subordination (sexually and in general). Although the ancient Egyptian culture was most probably not the most misogynist in the ancient Near East, as the position of women in Egyptian society appears to have been higher than in other settings, this society too promoted ideologies of masculine domination. One basic dogma expressed in multiple texts and images is: women are to be dominated, sexually, and politically. This cannot be questioned as it is their "nature". Therefore, it is also "natural" to exclude women (and feminised persons in general) from all social areas that confer dominance and power.

If we look back from here to the case of Hatshepsut we not only better understand her problem with being considered a legitimate king, we also understand better the critical function of the pornographic graffito mentioned above. Penetration is the sacrament of masculine domination in linking the public and the personal body. Therefore, it makes sense to show Hatshepsut as the feminine (i.e. subjugated) object of masculine sexuality. Being penetrated links the masculine public body of a woman king with the feminine personal body and destroys sacramentally the masculinity of the public body and with it the indispensable basis of Hatshepsut's rule.

The Greek Zeus-Syndrome

Characterising Greek culture as rape culture is not a malicious insinuation. The Greek mythical tales are so full of rape stories that it is not possible to name all the sources here. In contrast to ancient Egypt where the topic of violent sexuality is more or less limited to the realm of gods and kings, we find it in Greece on a broader level, including when it comes to dominating other men sexually. One of the well-known elements of Greek culture is the erotic relationship between an adult man (*erastes*) and a boy/adolescent (*eromenos*) between 12 and 17 years old, both from citizen families. However, this cultural institution of pederasty, limited in time and social range, is not as relevant here, as one might expect. Firstly, the sources depict it as a consensual[10] and instructive relationship; secondly, it implies erotic emotions;[11] and thirdly, pederasty – at least theoretically – avoids penetration. Therefore, depictions of pederast relationships do not typify the dynamics that are my focus in this chapter, namely, the traces of rape and other forms of gendered domination. The only characteristics that link pederasty to this can be seen in the clear hierarchy in terms of social status, as well as in the pains taken to avoid feminising the *eromenos* too much as this would compromise his honour as a future free man. If the free citizens of a Greek polis wanted to penetrate, dominate, or feminise someone, a slave or prostitute (male or female) would have been the object of choice. As long as the higher-ranking man was the penetrator, sexual intercourse with a male would not affect his masculinity, because sexual identity was defined by the role (i.e. dominant or submissive) in intercourse and not by the gender of the person penetrated. Where we see this hierarchy most clearly is in male-male sexual penetration in warfare.

56 *Why One Must Not Turn a Man into a Woman*

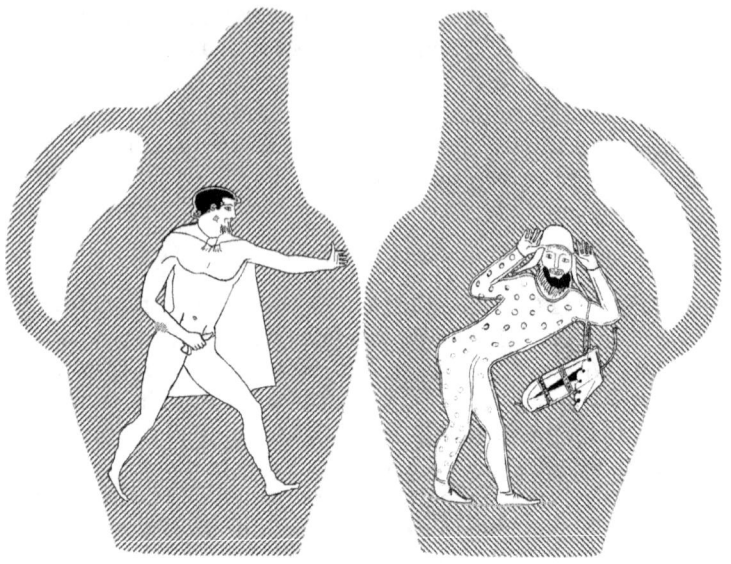

Figure 3.2 The "Eurymedon-vase"[12]

A famous visual representation of this phenomenon is the "Eurymedon-vase", an *oinochoe* (wine jug) dating from the time after the Persian wars, around 460 BCE (Figure 3.2).

The vase-painting refers to the Greek victory over Persian forces at the River of Eurymedon and celebrates this triumph with an icon of sexual domination.

The vase bears an inscription, nowadays almost invisible. The recent reconstruction of it reads: "I am Eurymedon, (but) you stand bent over" (Gerleigner 2016: 184). The text, attributed to the rapist (left), depicted as naked save for a cloak and clutching, in place of a weapon of war (a spear, or sword) his erect penis, links politics and sexual activity.

Many interpreters "saw this Athenian image as a metaphorical but at the same time relatively straight-forward representation of the military victory in the form of a Greek about to rape a Persian" (Gerleigner 2016: 177). The defeated soldier (on the right), *pars pro toto* representing the Persian army, or even the "barbarian East",[13] is already feminised by losing the battle. His subjugation is now completed by being penetrated by a Greek man (on the left). However, recent research also points out that the Greek attacker is depicted more like an auxiliary soldier of lower status. Gerleigner (2016: 177) concludes, "an Athenian citizen looking at the image could on the one hand distance himself from the base act of raping a submissive barbarian/.../but on the other hand appreciate the allusion to the victory, thus enjoying his superiority over both figures". Although one could ask if raping an enemy was something a Greek citizen needed to distance from, this interpretation may be true. I would, however, add that the fact that the penetrator is depicted as a Greek of lower status aggravates the humiliation of the defeated Persian: even the least of the Greeks is more powerful than a Persian. Additionally, "by making the aggressor the sole speaker of statements referring to both figures, the vase-painter further emphasised the figure's dominant role; it is he who assigns the archer his place, while the latter is deprived even of the voice to point out his position of submission" (Gerleigner 2016: 184). This message highlights and asserts the supremacy of Greek masculinity and feminises the defeated enemy.

The dishonouring of the defeated enemy is enhanced yet more by representing him with a comical attitude, which expresses "feminine" fear and helplessness. Hence, he holds up his hands over his head, fingers splayed, eyes opened very wide, his quiver dangling uselessly from his arm. At the same time, the turning of the back towards the penetrator and the bend at the waist can be interpreted as offering himself for penetration. This implies utter humiliation as in the Greek code of violent sexuality a man showing willingness or pleasure in being penetrated, loses all his masculinity and is completely feminised (cf. Reinsberg 1989: 192). Usually it is seen as the "natural" role of women to be helpless, weak, and dominated (not only) sexually by men. On the other hand, it is the masculine role to penetrate, to be strong and to dominate (not only sexually).

The manliest man in this sense is Zeus, the highest god, whose hegemonic sexuality is the prototype for the concept of rape culture (and, therefore, gave the name to this book as well).

Zeus needs no consent; he simply takes his sexual objects without asking. Whether the object of his desire is male (like Ganymede) or female (like Europa, Leda and many more) does not matter: alongside his preeminent masculinity all others are rendered feminine; all are weak humans and can be dominated by him easily.

While European history of art, as already mentioned in the introduction, often tends to cover up the brutal force of Zeus's sexual acts, ancient sources are less shy to display the encounter with the highest god as an experience of being overwhelmed and subjugated. This can be seen clearly, when paintings like Michelangelo's "Leda and the Swan",[14] depicting a rather coy Leda, turning her head away from a pleading looking swan, are compared with much more physical ancient pieces, like the terracotta oil lamp in Munich,[15] where Leda is fighting to keep the swan away with her arm, or the marble relief in London,[16] where swan-Zeus is menacingly grasping Leda's neck from above.

Although some ancient sources also ignore or downplay the rape character of the sexual encounter, the tendency to attribute characteristics of erotic seduction to the act is much more notable under Christian influence. Ancient sources have less of a problem with the implied domination and even seem to foreground it,[17] which is understandable when reckless sexuality is legitimised and celebrated by religious tradition. Mythical tradition portrays Zeus and also his son Herakles as strong men who show their supremacy by "taking women" without asking them. This is not surprising in a cultural context where a bride is given by her father to her husband. That Zeus and Herakles not even ask fathers or husbands when they seize the women they desire signifies reckless acts of disregard for human order. They can do so because they are strong enough to impose their will as their own law. In acting like this they show their superiority.

Adultery is not an ethical problem for a god; it is simply a display of his super-human power. What is forbidden to normal men is allowed for the most powerful who can do whatever they want as there is nobody who can hinder them – not even a divine wife, like Hera, although she tries again and again. Monogamy may be the recommended practice but the theory behind marriage is polygamous. Even a Greek man cannot break his own marriage (e.g. through sexual activities with lower-ranking women and men) as he has no obligation of fidelity to his wife.[18] He can only assault the sexual rights of other men by having sex with their daughters or wives, without permission. If a god wants to prove his superior power through sexual acts, the bold imperviousness to others' rights is a suitable means. Thus, a god can feminise human men without even penetrating them. A god-man who is able to rape a father's daughter or a husband's wife forces these men into a powerless position that effects a feminisation of their public body and shows the true, superior masculinity of the rapist. If the object is a father's son, the message is even stronger.[19]

The choice of the object does not say anything about the "sexual orientation" of the dominant man, as in the context of the Zeus-syndrome the sexual identity of the rapist is always defined as masculine by the power he exerts. On the other hand, every person's public body is defined as feminine through the domination they are subjected to. "Any penetration, if vaginal, anal or oral, is aiming on an object *defined* as feminine",[20] as Reinsberg (1989: 192) rightly observes. In my terminology: the gender of the public body of a penetrated person is always feminine, no matter if their personal body is male or female. Thus, when Zeus rapes Ganymede, Zeus is not "homosexual" in the modern sense, even if he is erotically attracted by the boy's beautiful body. Instead, this body although male in a biological sense is perceived on the level of the public body as feminine. Zeus is behaving like the *erastes* in the Greek polis, just that he does not need to bribe the boy with gifts; he simply takes what he likes. Sexuality as defined by the Zeus-syndrome is often just a game of power that has not much to do with lust or pleasure and nothing with love.

Violent sexuality in the framework of the Zeus-syndrome understands and uses the penis as a weapon and assimilates it symbolically with the spear, the arrow, or the sword. Similar meaning is attributed to the penetration with the penis as to the penetration with a weapon in war or hunting. Sexuality is a kind of battle or hunt, and war or hunting receive erotic undertones. In both sex and warfare, the penetrated object is seen as a kind of trophy. When Alexander rams his spear into the conquered country's soil, the message is that the victor has taken the territory as his property, much as a husband "takes" or "claims" his wife through intercourse. And, after winning a battle, the triumph can be completed by raping the defeated enemy.

Rome Dominates the World – A Man Dominates Rome

Although the relations and intersections of Greek and Roman cultures were very tight over centuries, one should not overlook the differences between the two, which can be noted also when it comes to rape culture. While the presence of Roman women in the public sphere is much higher than that of women in classical Greek contexts, there is no Roman institution comparable to pederasty, for instance. If a Roman man wanted to have sex with another man, he was free to use a slave or prostitute, that is, someone of lower rank; but social hierarchy had to be maintained. "Unlike most Greek states, Rome never idealised or even sanctioned homosexual relations with a freeborn youth, but generally condoned them with male slaves, who were in many cases boys, but in other cases were adults,/.../sexual service was a necessity for a slave and a 'duty' for a freed slave, regardless of age. We have more than one story of Roman soldiers being approached by commanders for sexual favors/.../. The general (and short-lived Emperor) Galba was said to have preferred very masculine-looking soldiers as his sexual partners" (Hubbard 2014: 150).

Sexual intercourse between men *per se* was not, seemingly, a big topic. Compared with Greek tradition, Roman upper-class society did not talk much about this – at least, we do not have sources comparable to the many depictions of male-male intercourse in Greek vase-painting. There is, however, one exception to this general observation. When Roman social order was not represented properly by the roles in sexual intercourse, political interest was aroused and debate ensued.

In the time when Roman imperialism dominated the Mediterranean world more and more, the republican state model

Why One Must Not Turn a Man into a Woman   61

seemed outdated and many prominent Roman politicians tried to introduce an autocratic system of rule. Exactly in this time, we have a debate on masculinity and sexual behaviour. Gaius Julius Caesar (100–44 BCE), one of the elite men fighting for a new system of government, was said to have been penetrated by a foreign king. In 80 BCE, when Caesar was around 20 years old, he was sent on a diplomatic mission to the court of Nicomedes (IV Philopator) who was the king of Bithynia[21] (94–74 BCE). The Roman historiographer C. Suetonius Tranquillus writes in his "Lives of the Caesars"[22]:

> *a quo, [i.e. Thermus] ad accersendam classem in Bithyniam missus desedit apud Nicomeden, non sine rumore prostratae regi pudicitiae;*
> Being sent by him [i.e. Thermus] to Bithynia to fetch the fleet, he spent much time with Nicomedes, not without the rumour of having given his chastity to the king.
> (Suetonius, Caesar 2)[23]

According to Suetonius, the rumours arising from Caesar's early stay at Bithynia were used against him by his opponents in the struggle for power. Suetonius, who was himself a follower of republican ideas and not very fond of autocracy, dedicates the complete paragraph 49 of his "Life of Julius Caesar" to this topic, quoting several demeaning sayings. Caesar was called "mattress of the royal bed", "brothel of Bithynia", and "Bithynian queen", to name only a few. Suetonius closes his paragraph by quoting verses that the soldiers who followed Caesar's chariot dared to sing[24] during the triumphal procession celebrating the victory over Gallia:

> *Gallias Caesar subegit, Nicomedes Caesarem;*
> Caesar vanquished the Gallias, Nicomedes vanquished Caesar;
> *Ecce Caesar nunc triumphat, qui subegit Gallias:*
> See Caesar now in triumph, who vanquished the Gallias,
> *Nicomedes non triumphat, qui subegit Caesarem.*
> Nicomedes does not triumph, who vanquished Caesar.
> (Suetonius, Caesar 49,4)

62 Why One Must Not Turn a Man into a Woman

The political dimension of the rumour that Caesar had allowed the Bithynian king to use him as his lover boy, comes out very clearly in the soldiers' song, which links military victory and sexuality by comparing the defeated enemies directly with the penetrated Caesar. The crassly comical element of the verses stems from the contrast between the utmost manly victor who was able to subjugate all the Gallic tribes and his having been subjugated himself by penetration. The femininity of a penetrated man is in stark contrast to the masculinity of a general winning a war. But for the elite politicians (like Cicero), defending the republican system (and the privileges their families enjoyed under this system) against the autocratic attack of Caesar, this contrast was much more than a joke. It was as serious reproach and a political tool that could be used to fight Caesar's monarchic ambitions. A man whose public body was feminised by playing the feminine role in sexual intercourse to a king who was dependent on Rome cannot be allowed to dominate the Roman Empire. Only a "true man" with a supremely masculine political public body could be appropriate for ruling the supreme power of the Mediterranean world. Although the argument comes from people who think that Rome should be dominated by the Senate as a collegium of masculine peers and not by one single person, discrediting Caesar by attributing a feminine public body to him makes sense. If Caesar can be depicted as "just a woman", then the most dangerous enemy of the traditional system is declared incapable to rule because of his lack of masculinity. His supporters are meant to understand that they are following a feminine person, unfit to rule, who in Roman tradition exemplifies a shameful and "unnatural" perversion of the social order.

Suetonius (Vita Caesarum, Divus Iulius 22) tells that Caesar, after having conquered Gallia, boasted that from now on he will dominate all of his opponents. When someone replied that this would be difficult for a woman, he jokingly referred to the (mythical) examples of successful female rulers (Semiramis and the Amazons). If we can trust this report, Caesar tried to react to the reproach that his political body is feminine by separating his public body from his personal body. He does so by referring to powerful women, who despite their personal body being feminine, gained dominant masculinity in their public body. The argument presupposes that Caesar's sexual activity relates to his personal body only, while his public body is clearly masculine. It is highly improbable that this argument was seen as convincing. Firstly, it implies that the rumours about the affair with Nicomedes are true, and secondly, this splitting of the two bodies cannot work politically. Once a sexual act has become "a topic" in public discourse, it cannot be reduced to a private matter anymore – especially not in a culture where sexuality is regarded as something highly relevant to the social order. Additionally, one should keep in mind that Caesar visited the king of Bithynia not as a private person. He came to his court in an official public function. Therefore, the attempt of reducing any affair to the personal body alone could not be plausible.

The topic also played a role in other politicians' careers. Augustus, basing his political status on the adoption by Caesar, was accused by his opponent Marc Antony (and others) of being feminised and having paid for this adoption with shameful sexual "service" (*stuprum*) for his uncle Caesar (Suetonius, Vita Caesarum, Augustus 68). Additionally, Suetonius (Vita Caesarum, Nero 29) tells that Nero, one of the favourite targets of republican critique, was feminised by letting himself be penetrated – even by slaves (cf. Hubbard 2014: 150). With this obvious upturning of the proper social order, Nero, otherwise conducting himself like an oriental god-king, proves himself incapable of dominating the Roman Empire. A man who admits that a lower-class man uses his personal body like a feminine one cannot claim the highest masculinity for his public body.

Instead, the emperor as the man of men should show his supreme masculinity by dominating others both sexually and politically. That is what most of the rulers did – in spite of all the rumours of feminisation. If Augustus abducts elite women from their husbands,[25] it might constitute a bit of a moral problem, but this is a manifestation of the hierarchy of power of the Zeus-syndrome. Caligula increased the recklessness of sexual domination by "taking" not only the wives but also the sons of upper-class families (Vita Caesarum, Caligula 36). Additionally, he abuses senators by using them as personal servants during his banquets (Vita Caesarum, Caligula 26,2). They had to wear a dress characteristic for young slaves who had to display their beauty (including their private parts) while serving at the banquet. Just like their mythical prototype Ganymede, they were offered as sexual objects to the drinking men.[26] By using senators as his "Ganymede", the emperor clearly shows which kind of hierarchy he has in mind: he is one of the gods, while even the noblest men belong to his human underlings.[27] Nero is said to have followed this example, even (blasphemously) extending his sexual rapaciousness to Vestal Virgins (Vita Caesarum, Nero 28).[28] Of course, ignoring human and divine laws will have incited fury among the traditional nobility but it is also a bold expression of Zeus-syndrome. The mightiest man, representing the gods[29] by dominating the world, can have sex with whomever he wants. Neither humans nor gods can hinder him.

If we look at our present from the material analysed in this chapter, we can better understand how masculine domination, the hateful contempt for penetrated men, and misogynist attitudes relate to one another. Even if religion nowadays seems to be of less importance in public discourse than it was in ancient times, the Zeus-syndrome and its effects on the public and personal bodies of men and women remains powerful. Even in "secular" societies, this specific politico-religious amalgam influences the understanding of masculinities so much that even conservative-to-fundamentalist US Christians do not shrink from supporting a "Grab-'em-by-the-pussy"-President.[30] On the other hand, one could imagine their reaction if the Kremlin were to publish a video showing their hero penetrated by a Russian callboy ... The reverberations of the Zeus-syndrome are alive and well.

Notes

1 The complete text of the tale can be found in Lichtheim (1976: 214–223). For the English translation of the paragraph, see Lichtheim (1976: 219–220). Matić (2021: 74–75) gives a short summary of the story. The original papyrus can be admired at: https://viewer.cbl.ie/viewer/object/Pap_1_2/8/LOG_0000/ (accessed 13/04/2022).

Why One Must Not Turn a Man into a Woman 65

2 Junge (1995: 933) sees aspects of a satirical critique of the political situation, characterised by weak kings and a court administration that is blocked by selfishness and wicked cabals.
3 Housed in the Egyptian Museum (JE32169 and CG14716); a picture can be found at: https://commons.wikimedia.org/wiki/File:Narmer_Palette.jpg (accessed 13/04/2022).
4 English translation is taken from Lichtheim (1975: 231). Explanations [in brackets] are my own. For the complete story, see Lichtheim (1975: 222–235).
5 Theriomorphic depictions of the king are not just allegories. Instead, they refer to super-human abilities of the ruler and associate him with other gods whose super-human power is also expressed by animal or hybrid appearance.
6 Bull Palette, greywacke, 3300–3100 BCE. Louvre Museum, accession number E 11255. Graphic based on comparing https://commons.wikimedia.org/wiki/File:Fran%C3%A7oise_Foliot_-_Palette_au_taureau.jpg [accessed 13/04/2022] (HD photo) with Schroer (2005: 223, fig. 122 – drawing), and private material, created by the author.
7 Here, the word "sacrament" is not used theologically but in the broader sense of a sign which performs what it signifies. In this sense, a sacrament creates a space where its general meaning happens and can be experienced in a specific case.
8 In contrast to this ideal, the reality of autocratic states is characterised by the necessity of consent-building – at least within the elite power-machinery through which the monarch exerts his rule, e.g. among heads of military and administration.
9 As the personal body implies the physical body and the self-perception of it, one could, of course, assume that the personal body might also be feminised in a way, but this depends very much on the psychological and cultural conditions which cannot be properly analysed here.
10 For modern readers the notion that a 12-year-old boy can give informed consent to a relationship with a considerably older man is, of course, more than questionable. As pederasty was a sociocultural institution comparable to a *rite de passage*, it seems not very probable that Athenian boys had any option to avoid this kind of relationships if they were the legitimate son of a free citizen. Yet, they definitely had the freedom of choosing among several *erastes*-candidates.
11 The emotions are, however, one-sided. While the adult *erastes* is allowed to fall in love with the chosen boy, the boy is expected to remain impassive, even when it comes to sexual intercourse (cf. Reinsberg 1989: 194–196).

12 Graphic adapted from https://sammlungonline.mkg-hamburg. de/de/object/Oinochoe-Eurymedon-Kanne-oder-Perser-Kanne/ 1981.173/dc00126657 (accessed 13/04/2022) and created by the author. For a 3D scan, see https://www.fdr.uni-hamburg.de/record/ 871#.YeWsHfgxl3g (accessed 13/04/2022).
13 Gerleigner (2016: 168): "Several attributes the figure is wearing belong to the typical iconography used to depict 'Eastern barbarians' (from a Greek perspective) in late archaic and early classical Athenian vase-painting: the rounded cap with cheekflaps ('Phrygian cap'), the patterned body suit (with long sleeves and trouser legs), the (pointed and laced) shoes, and the bow-and-arrow quiver hanging from his left upper-arm".
14 For the London painting (a copy after the lost original, after 1530, inventory number NG1868) cf. https://www.nationalgallery. org.uk/paintings/after-michelangelo-leda-and-the-swan (accessed 13/04/2022).
15 https://commons.wikimedia.org/wiki/File:Staatliche_ Antikensammlungen_M%C3%BCnchen_896.JPG (accessed 13/04/2022). See also the similar motif on a sarcophagus from Beit Shearim (ca. 200 CE; now Rockefeller Museum, Jerusalem): https://commons.wikimedia.org/wiki/File:Leda_and_the_ Swan_-_Beit_Shearim.jpg (accessed 13/04/2022).
16 The relief from Argos (Greece) is part of the British Museum's collection (number 1973,0302.1) (cf. https://www.britishmuseum. org/collection/object/G_1973-0302-1) (accessed 13/04/2022).
17 Otherwise it would not make sense to use the topic as a decorative motif on everyday objects.
18 This statement, of course, does not preclude that wives would not fight to restrict the sexual libertinism of their husbands. Cohen (2014: 190–191) even mentions that a wife imprisoned her husband at home to prevent sexual intercourse with a female slave. Additionally, the mother of the husband, if widowed and living in the same household, might also control the sexual behaviour of her son.
19 Of course, the Zeus-syndrome may be found in other cultures also. The name is, however, justified in my own context, because, alongside the Bible, the classical Greek traditions are particularly formative for Western cultures where the phenomenon has found its continuation in phenomena that can be associated with stories of Zeus and Herakles.
20 The English translation is my own.
21 Bithynia was one of the less important kingdoms originating from Alexander's empire. It covered a strip of Anatolia's (then *Asia Minor*) coast with the Black Sea.
22 A well-readable translation is given by Edwards (2000).

Why One Must Not Turn a Man into a Woman 67

23 My quotations of Suetonius's Latin text follow Martinet (2006); the English translations are my own.
24 Singing songs with abusive remarks about the *triumphator* was commonplace in the Roman triumphal procession (*pompa triumphalis*).
25 Suetonius reports that Augustus was known to have committed numerous acts of adultery, disrespecting the honour of both husbands and their wives (Vita Caesarum, Augustus 69).
26 The Ganymede-role of these servants obviously was common as it is mentioned in several sources, even in Roman and Jewish critique (cf. Vössing 2004: 514–517).
27 Vössing (2004: 437) very convincingly interprets the political career of Caligula's horse in this line. If even a horse can be Senator, there can be no doubt of that the Senate is obsolete.
28 Of course, this act of blasphemy would have caused bitter critique by many citizens. Yet, only later authors could dare to speak out against it by using this atrocity as one element of their puzzle portraying Nero as a mad tyrant (as they did with Caligula and Domitian also). Yet, if an emperor really wanted to follow the Hellenistic god-king ideology the behaviour could even be seen as appropriate. Zeus did not fear Hera, why should the god Nero fear Vesta?
29 The Roman philosopher Seneca (De Clementia I 1,2) invited Nero to understand himself as *deorum vice*.
30 See https://www.nytimes.com/2016/10/08/us/donald-trump-tape-transcript.html (accessed 26/01/2022).

4 Defending Masculinity Under Oppression
The Biblical Plan to Be Different

The Historical Setting and the Quest for "Israel"

What do we mean by the term "Israel"? Jacob? The group Moses leads out from Egypt? The united monarchy of David and Solomon? The kingdom in the North, later destroyed by the Assyrian empire? The kingdom in the South that adopts the traditions of the northern kingdom after its destruction? The new "state" after the end of the Babylonian exile? In the Hebrew Bible, the term "Israel" can signify all of these (cf. Wagner 2012). Hence, if we try to use the term in any historical context, we have to decide how we use it. Historically speaking, both the exodus-group and the United Kingdom of David and Solomon (cf. Finkelstein & Silberman 2007) are seen more and more as fictitious constructions of the past by later generations. As can be concluded from extra-biblical sources, "Israel" was indeed the name of the northern kingdom in the region around Samaria with kings like Ahab, Omri, Joram, and Jehu of the 9th-century BCE (cf. Schipper 2021: 34–54).[1] After the conquest of Samaria by Neo-Assyrian forces in 722/720 BCE the term "Israel" most probably began to signify something more than the northern kingdom, because from then on Judah, the southern kingdom around Jerusalem, adopted the identity of the annihilated kingdom in the north and even appropriated it for the construction of a common past. Later Judah was also defeated and parts of the Judean elite were exiled to Babylon. However, due to the pre-exilic integration of Israel's northern tradition into the southern collective memory, the group returning from exile to the Persian province of Yehud identified themselves as "Israel", and the return from Babylon as something like a re-enactment of ancient "Israel" returning triumphantly and liberated from Egypt. To clarify my terminology: based on the historically relevant sources, I use "Israel" of the northern kingdom of the 9th and 8th centuries BCE and "Yehud" to refer to the post-exilic political unit around Jerusalem. I also use "Israel" for the collective identity constructed by biblical authors, while acknowledging that this does not pertain to a historical, ontological entity.

The situation of the Yehud was not only, or even chiefly, shaped by the end of the Babylonian Empire and the return of large numbers of descendants of the upper classes who had been deported during the Exile. Instead, this appears to be rather inflated, or misrepresented, in the biblical narratives. As Bernd U. Schipper states, "the archaeological record rules out the possibility of a mass return. Neither Jerusalem nor Yehud shows evidence of a spike in settlement growth in the early Persian period. A more realistic number of returnees would be around 4,000 people coming back to Yehud over several decades" (Schipper 2021: 75). The Yehud was also characterised by the experience of being unimportant and powerless. The region of Yehud with its estimated 12,000–30,000 inhabitants (cf. Schipper 2021: 75), constituting a small and rather insignificant part of the Persian Empire, was thrown into competition with diverse other religious and cultural traditions that were interpreted as spelling deadly peril to the precarious identity of the conservative authors and editors of post-exilic texts. In response they tried to assert (and thereby establish) the identity of a post-exile Yehud as legitimate heir of "Israel", understood not so much as a state but as an ethno-religious entity: as the one and only YHWH-people, the "holy seed", and as completely distinct from all other peoples.

Leviticus and the Masculinity of the Men of "Israel"

As we have seen above, in Greek and Roman societies dominant men were to some degree and with circumscriptions free to use a male of lower status as sexual object. In the Hebrew Bible, however, we find general rules proscribing male-male penetration. Such sexual intercourse is called an "abomination" (Lev. 18:22, 20:13), usually understood as an acutely pejorative judgement[2] that has become highly influential in the Christian debate on "homosexuality" – even though it is anachronistic to compare man-to-man-sex in antiquity with the modern concept of "gay" orientation, identity, and relationship,[3] as I showed in the previous chapter. The most relevant regulations are in the book of Leviticus. Very literally, these translate as follows[4]:

Lev 18:22
You shall not lie with a male the lyings of a woman. An abomination is it.

Lev 20:13
If a man lies with a male the lyings of a woman, they have committed an abomination both; they shall surely die to death. Their blood is upon them.

Both texts are part of the "Holiness Code" (Leviticus 18–26) which is a collection of legal regulations. Containing older material, the code most probably was supplemented and redacted in post-exilic time, in the period of the Persian Yehud. Compared with the power of the Persian king and his satraps, in evidence all over the Empire, "Israel" had every reason to feel powerless and weak.[5] Through a strategy of othering,[6] the Holiness Code works on the problem of social inferiority and precarious identity. Here, the dominated ones are not defined as victims of oppression; instead, they constitute the chosen people of the only God while all others (worshipping non-existing deities) have no part in him. By depicting and elevating "Israel" as a zone of holiness, the authors try to establish a *de facto* national identity in the absence of a nation state. The tiny spot of Judah, one of the most marginal areas in the vast Persian Empire, should be understood as the centre of creation, a stronghold of holy otherness. Banning penetration/penetrated males from this holy area can now be understood as one way of symbolically disenfranchising the hierarchical structure of the empire. All Jewish men are united in equal holiness and, as such, different from all pagan men who are not holy (cf. Seidl 2009).

Both Leviticus 18:22 and 20:13 focus on male-male penetration without any reference to such concepts as love, sexual orientation, reproduction, or identity. The reason why Israel's God is said to be against such acts can be deduced from the specific expression "with a male as with a woman". The word "male" is broader than "man" and includes men, boys, male slaves, and any other persons (or even animals) defined as masculine. The man addressed in the Levitical regulations should abstain from using *any* male as sexual object. The way these regulations are formulated indicates that their wider context is one of masculine domination, where all males are superior to all females. Obviously, these texts presuppose a cultural framework where a man of status decides with whom he has sexual intercourse. The divine will, however, limits his freedom of choice by excluding any male. The men of Israel/Judah are obliged to limit their sexual activity to women only. They are not allowed to treat males sexually like women. It is likely that the act to be avoided is sexual penetration, which is reserved for encounters with women. That sexual intercourse with women is alluded to here makes it obvious that the problem lies with penetrating a male person. This is deemed to be against the divine order as it would change, or compromise, the gender of a male. Penetration of the personal body feminises the public body, and so the penetrated male is "turned into a woman" by being treated as a woman. In a cultural world where the masculine gender is associated with domination, strength, and the power to rule, while the feminine gender is associated with being dominated, helpless, weak, needing guidance and protection by a man, it must appear as a crime to reduce a male person (be it a boy, a man, or a slave) to a lower status by treating him like a woman.

This concept can also be found in Genesis 19, where Lot saves his male visitors from gang rape by offering the aggressive mob his virgin daughters instead. When the men of Sodom try to rape Lot's guests, Lot acts like a protective host – if not like a protective father! – by offering substitute victims. In ancient Near Eastern societies this would not have been a simple solution for a father, as it was a matter of his own paternal honour to preserve the virginity of his daughters until marriage. Lot's substitution has not only to do with codes of hospitality but also with the implied gender problem. It seems that the sexual abuse of male strangers causes much greater damage than the violation of Lot's own virgin daughters. This is so because of the cultural perception that females are "naturally made" for penetration, while males are not. The story in Genesis 19 also indicates that penetration was expressive of power (cf. Gunda 2010: 270–271). The father decides on the sexual use of his daughters without asking. Later their husbands would decide when to penetrate without asking. And also, the men who want to gang rape the strangers want to use penetration as a tool to put men of lower status in their subservient place in the social hierarchy. While this reckless and violent behaviour is attributed to men of Sodom,[7] it may be suspected that the story was also told with a view to imparting to men of Judah/Israel that the penetration of other men conferred dominance on the penetrator and humiliation on the penetrated. This suspicion becomes a well justified one, when we look at the story in Judges 19, where Israelite men try to rape an Israelite visitor. Just like the men of Sodom they are offered female victims as substitutes. In contrast to the story in Genesis 19, the aggressors at Gibeah violate the Levite's wife in place of their original target: namely, the male Levite guest. As there are no angels at hand to save the poor woman, she is raped the whole night long and does not survive this "phallic aggression" (cf. Gunda 2010: 272–280).

If rape of men by men occurred within "Israel" also, as Judges 19 suggests, we can understand that the Leviticus regulations in particular and the Holiness Code more generally, had implications for social justice. It states that no male within the group should be humiliated by being used "like a woman". This ideal of equality among males was not unique in the ancient Near East (cf. Hieke 2015: 23–25). Even if this exclusion of sexual aggression[8] within a group of equal men might have been no more than an ideal, it still could be used to make a difference between "Israel", the chosen people, and the other peoples, where powerful men had less or no restriction to use penetration of lower men as a means to manifest their power. The virtual zone of holy otherness grants a masculine public body to males of "Israel" and allows them to understand themselves as real men. Male-male penetration is banned from the zone of holy otherness as such penetration would annihilate the collective masculinity of" Israel" and assimilate God's people to other peoples, where powerful men's sexual rights were less restricted. Thus, the tabooing of male-male sex contributes effectively to the creation of corporate identity through othering. Related to the idea of holiness is also the death penalty, which is conferred not only on the penetrating man but also the penetrated male (Lev 20:13). To punish, conceivably, a victim of male-male rape is clearly against modern ethics. In the framework of holiness, however, ethical sensibilities are not the major point. The supreme value is the holy purity of God's people. A man turned into a woman by being penetrated is as disturbing to holiness as his abuser, and that is why both of them must die.[9]

The strategy of othering can be found all over the Holiness Code. Other peoples are doing evil things, but "Israel" will not do such (see Lev 18:1–5, below). "Abomination" is one of the central expressions for taboos, which separate God's own people from others. The dietary rules, reducing communication with the non-Jewish world by excluding the possibility of eating together, belong to this strategy also. They function as identity markers and help towards creating corporate identity by making a difference between Judah/Israel and the rest of the world. Israel is holy, different from the profane world of the pagans, not only by avoiding abomination-food but also by avoiding abomination-sex.

If we want to understand better what the strategy of the Holiness Code is about, we should take a short look at the socio-historical setting of the text. Although in the narrated world God speaks to Moses between the liberation from Egyptian slavery and entering the Promised Land, the text is not that old. The chronology is not a historical one but has symbolic value. Israel is in a situation of between-ness: between deliverance from Egypt and entry to Canaan. Both Egypt and Canaan are depicted as locales where foreign norms, rules, and values dominate the lives of unholy people and create a way of life alien to God's people. This setting is clearly expressed:

> [1] Then YHWH spoke to Moses, saying, [2] "Speak to the sons of Israel and say to them,
> 'I, YHWH, (am) your God.
> [3] 'According to the practices of the land Egypt where you lived, do not act,
> and according to the practices of the land Canaan where I am bringing you, do not act;
> you shall not follow *their* regulations.
> [4] Perform *my* justice-orders and keep *my* commands, to live according to them;
> I, YHWH, (am) your God.
> [5] So, keep *my* commands and *my* justice-orders,
> which, if one does them, one lives by them;
> I (am) YHWH.
>
> (Lev 18:1–5)

The text declares the identity of God to be the source and the guarantor for the identity of "Israel". As long as the people follow his will, they are his people. As the people's god is different from others, the identity of his people is different from other peoples'. The others' way of life must not be adopted by the YHWH-people. "Israel" has to differ from Canaan as from Egypt. Interestingly, Canaan with its different culture is seen here as being as dangerous as Egypt and appears not so much as Promised Land. Rather, it is connected with dangerous seduction and religio-cultural alienation. This indicates that the text does not presuppose a situation where the YHWH-people and their way of life are dominating this country. Instead, the Holiness Code presupposes a time, when "Israel" had to live under foreign rule – most probably Persian rule, as already indicated. YHWH's people is holy by being different from others. It is a heterotopia, an alternative space to the culture and religion of the mainstream. Canaan/Yehud cannot be left like Egypt, as it is the land given by God (for the returning group, now for the second time). Therefore, it is necessary to construct a spiritual exodus within the land by means of a different way of life: "Israel" believes and lives differently; they eat different food and practise sexuality in a way different from others. In addition to constructing and strengthening identity as "otherness", the alternative sexual norm of not penetrating males constructs a masculine public body for the "sons of Israel". They build up a collective of peers, who do not penetrate each other. They will respect each other's masculinity and not turn any male (not even boys or slaves) into women. Thus, a masculine public body is constructed for the "sons of Israel", a body free and independent, arising from protecting their personal body from being dominated sexually.

We cannot know as to how far this programme was effective in practice, yet what we can say is that this idea of masculinity, even if it would have succeeded in protecting non-consenting men of lower status from being victimised sexually, the concept would not protect the enemy, who can be assaulted sexually.[10] It also did not imply much, if any, progress for women. The reason is quite simple: women must be excluded from the ideal of equality, to support the "logic" of masculine domination, whereby it is necessary for the masculinity of holy-equal men that there be someone they can dominate, in order to enact, assert, and stabilise their masculinity. If male objects (at least sexually) are excluded, then, in a binary worldview, females are the only objects left for sexual domination. Under the conditions of foreign colonial rule, the public body will not find much public space to exert its masculinity. The lack of power in politics, economics, and culture makes the patriarchal household the prominent space of domination for the "sons of Israel". It is here that the ideal father rules in his full masculinity like a king over his subordinates.[11]

Joseph and Potiphar's Wife: How a Beautiful Slave Defends His Masculinity

If foreign rule is conceived as an attack on collective masculinity, personal slavery is even worse, and being a foreigner's slave must be seen as complete feminisation. Even if one cannot say that every slaveholder sexually abused his slaves, it is true that in most cases he could do so without significant sanctions (cf. Cohen 2014). The question, how a "son of Israel" can maintain his masculinity under such circumstances, is one of the main topics of the "Joseph in Egypt" novella in the Hebrew Bible: especially in the story about Joseph and the wife of Egyptian Potiphar (Genesis 39).

As Joseph is Potiphar's slave, the wife of Joseph's master might plausibly think of herself as having some claim to enjoying the beautiful (Gen 39:6) body of this man. Whether her husband, too, acquired Joseph for sexual purposes, is not mentioned in the text, although there is a lot of speculation about this in its history of interpretation.[12] The wife of Potiphar is left nameless, and many modern readers find this insulting. It is, however, relevant for the narrative strategy of the text. Therefore, we cannot not fill this gap by giving the woman a name without impacting and distorting the message of the text. Anonymity in this instance seems to have the same effect as in the Gospel of John. As the mother[13] of Jesus as well as the "disciple whom Jesus loved"[14] have no name, their identity is formed exclusively by their relation to Jesus: mother and disciple. This is not a mistake; it gets to the heart of the identity and function of these narrative figures in the text. The wife of Potiphar is acting as the slaveholder's wife. This is her identity in the text and the basis for how she acts. The idea behind this is that a wife shares in the status and in the rights of her husband. This idea does not come "out of the blue". In a monogamous marriage, the wife's task was to control the male and female slaves in her husband's house. In such cases, she was acting as the boss of the household to organise housekeeping. Although the slaves were not her property, she could give orders in the name of her husband. Yet, a wife (ab)using slaves for sexual purposes posed a risk for husbands who expected their wives to be faithful. In much of the ancient Near East, while married men had some sexual freedom, married women were expected to confine their sexual activities to their husbands alone.[15] Anyway, the story tells that Potiphar's wife decided to use her husband's authority to use the beautiful slave for her own pleasure. As "his master's wife" (Gen 39:7), using the power of the slaveholder, she commands Joseph to have sex with her. In contrast to much of its reception history (cf. Küchler 1986: 149–154), the biblical text itself does not speak of any attempts to seduce, persuade, or cajole the man. Topics like romance, love, or relationship are out of sight. Johanna Stiebert rightly points out that the text portrays Potiphar's wife as "a privileged woman, the wife of a powerful man, who abuses her power over Joseph, a Hebrew slave, by commanding and pestering him for sex" (2019: 107). A master orders without waiting for consent and here so does the wife of the master. Her order is short and clear: "Lie down with me" (Gen 39:7,10). Although this order is repeated day by day (39:10), it does not meet with obedience. This detail in the text indicates that the intention of the woman to act as the powerful avatar of her husband fails.

If we look at the story from the perspective of gender roles, we see a fight for masculinity on both sides: the woman tries to masculinise her social body by acting dominantly and channelling her husband; the male slave defends his masculinity by refusing to obey or submitting his body. As the text does not indicate anything extra-ordinary[16] about the intended sexual intercourse, one can conclude that Joseph is expected to play the masculine, penetrating role. Therefore, the feminisation of his personal body is not an issue. Instead, his social body is at risk of being feminised by the sexual pressure of his master's wife who tries to dominate his physical personal body. In the cultural system of masculine domination, it is the man who decides whom to desire.[17] Usually, the woman has to be beautiful and attractive, so that the man will decide to be with her.[18] Potiphar's wife, however, is claiming masculine rights in trying to control the slave's beautiful body. At the same time, she is feminising his social body by forcing him into the position of rape victim (cf. Ebach 2007: 177). As the victim role is seen as typically feminine in the gendered system of masculine domination, it cannot be any surprise to find similarities between the Joseph narrative and the Tamar story in 2 Samuel 13. For example, Stiebert (2019: 84) rightly observes that among other intertextual links "both sexual violators – Potiphar's wife and Amnon – utter the same command: 'lie with me!' (39:7, 12; 2 Sam 13:11)". However, unlike Tamar who resists in vain and is victimised with bitter consequences, the man Joseph manages to escape the danger he is in. He successfully defends his sexual self-control and with it his masculinity.[19] His success has not only to do with the lack of physical strength of his master's wife, who cannot hold him tightly enough to seize more than his garment (Gen 39:12). After the master-woman's first attack, he resists by defending his sexual integrity (that is, his masculinity) also with powerful speech:[20]

> Look, my master does not care for anything in the house,
> and all which is to him, he gave it into my hand.
> No one (is) greater than me in this house
> and he excluded nothing from me except only you as you are his wife;
> how then could I do such great evil and sin before God?
> (Gen 39:8–9)

These are not the submissive words of a slave; this is how a free man and lord speaks. Joseph boldly defines his position of power and at the same time reduces the position of the woman, who is wanting to be master, to just being part of his master's property. Although Joseph's power derives from his master, "nobody" (not even his master?) limits his power in the house, which is the universe where he as well as his master's wife are active. Although Joseph's power does not yet reach the political sphere outside the house,[21] in this domestic sphere he *is* the only ruler. Also assuming the avatar of the absent and/or inactive master, Joseph decides over all of the property of his master. The fact that he has no authority over his master's wife does not mean that she can dominate him. She is just the one and only part of his master's possessions that is excluded from Joseph's authority. However, for Joseph, she does not share in her husband's power. Instead, she is under Potiphar's direct control while all other things owned by the master are to be controlled by Joseph. The slave defines himself as the *alter ego* of the master, sharing into his masculine public body – or even being part of his master's public body,[22] if we accept the idea of an extended public body. Although we do not find here any theory comparable with that of Paul's "being in Christ", the basic concept is similar insofar as a public body is seen as comprising more than one personal body. Anyway, Joseph does not allow the wife of his master to be a power avatar of her husband. She is part of her husband's belongings, owned by him exclusively. Therefore, it would be an evil thing for Joseph to be unfaithful to his master and a sin against the divine protector of patriarchal marriage (cf. e.g. Deuteronomy 5:21).[23] Realising the iron logic of masculine domination behind Joseph's boldly masculine speech, it cannot be a surprise to the reader that in the end, the woman decides to get Joseph out of the house. A master's wife, somehow sharing in his status, will not easily accept a slave telling her that she is only the property of her husband. Even if it is true in a way, she must feel insulted. Her scheming finally proves that Joseph is (temporarily) wrong. She is, indeed, able to share in the power of her husband by getting the slave removed and sent to prison. In the end, Joseph also was wrong concerning the power of his master. There is, indeed, someone "greater" in the house, and a slave is just a slave.

As already indicated above, my interpretation of this narrative is guided by the idea of a post-exile origin of Genesis 39. Indeed, recent research into the Joseph novella indicates quite clearly that the episode with Potiphar's wife belongs to the younger parts (cf. Römer 2019) of the Joseph story in Gen 37–50. Schipper analyses the Egyptian background of the Joseph novella and concludes: "The Egyptian background of the story about Joseph in Gen 37–50 does not point to the New Kingdom but to the Late Period Egypt" (2019: 23) and proposes to date the story to the Persian era. Therefore, it seems plausible to connect Genesis 39 with the above-mentioned sexual regulations in Leviticus. Both text groups belong to a similar socio-cultural context and react to it in similar ways. The masculinity of the "sons of Israel" is seen as being under attack by foreign rule – be it Persian or Ptolemaic.[24] While the Leviticus texts defend threatened masculinity by tabooing same-sex intercourse between men to avoid the existence of penetrated men in "Israel", Genesis 39 shows how to defend masculinity under the condition of slavery by declaring gender hierarchy as more important than slavery hierarchies.[25]

If we look at these texts from the perspective of modern readers, we have to concede that there is not much positive to take away from them, although critique of violent sexuality is not nothing. However, even the dark sides of a text can be helpful if only we decide to think and to act differently. For example, it can be helpful to understand that the disdain of penetrated men has to do with the disdain of women and femininity in general (cf. Greenough 2021: 24–26) – but we should not accept this gendered hierarchy or abusiveness. We can agree with the biblical rejection of sexual violence, although we need and ought to extend this to women, children, everyone. Even the most helpless and dependent person has the right to sexual integrity and autonomy – like Joseph, the slave in Genesis 39. Yet, we have to think about how this right can be realised and become more than an idea. *How* can societies and institutions guarantee sexual self-control in practice? *What* are the checks and balances that can effectively defend the powerless against sexual attacks of powerful men and women? The ancient texts begin to approach these questions but do not answer or resolve them.

Notes

1 The Egyptian Merneptah-Stele (1208 BCE), which mentions a group of people called "Israel", unfortunately, does not give much information about this group. Probably they were located in the North, more or less in the same region as the later northern kingdom (cf. Schipper 2021: 14–15).
2 In contrast to the traditional understanding, Lings (2009: 248) rightly states that "tô'evâ covers any abominable behaviour that makes the men and women of Israel stray from the way marked out for them by YHWH".
3 On the problems of applying the Leviticus regulations in contemporary times, see Nissinen (1998: 128–134), Gunda (2010: 256–312), and Hieke (2015).
4 I cannot follow Lings's translation/interpretation: "You shall not commit incest with any close relative, male or female" (2009: 249). Nothing in Leviticus 18:22 and 20:13 indicates a limitation to members of the same family. Lings's exegetical use of the

Defending Masculinity Under Oppression 81

incest topic is highly selective and not convincing. In addition, he unfortunately ignores the context of masculine domination.
5 If we try to express the power hierarchy in gendered language, the Persian king is the manliest of all men as he holds the highest power in the empire. His local representative in Judah is the most powerful (i.e. the most masculine) man in the satrapy. All the dominated local men are feminised in comparison with him.
6 Cf. Punt (2016). Although Punt focuses on the New Testament, his analysis is helpful for a broader understanding of othering (cf. also Kartzow 2009).
7 Notoriously, this has gone on to designate as "Sodomites" men practising same-sex intercourse.
8 Taken verbally, both Leviticus 18:22 and 20:13 exclude also consenting (i.e. non aggressive/violent) male-male sex, but this is not the focus. Both verses exclusively address the active partner in intercourse, while there is no rule for the male person who is to be penetrated. Although he also is condemned, the regulations do not address him as a subject of decision. There simply is nothing said like "you shall not allow a man to lie with you like with a woman".
9 The formula used in Leviticus 20:13 for the sanction of the death penalty does not make clear that the perpetrator and his victim are put to death by human authorities. Instead, it is probable that they die the socio-religious death of being dead to God, or ostracised.
10 Although the Hebrew Bible is not speaking about raping male enemies, sexualised violence can be found often. "The man who does not merely die by the sword, but who has his head cut off, his extremities amputated, or his foreskin sliced from his penis, is the victim of sexualized violence. Just as women can be sexually assaulted without penile penetration, so can men" (Thiede 2022: 74).
11 Daughters (and other family members) are not completely exempted from the sexual domination of the father (cf. Stiebert 2016).
12 Some later Jewish reception assumes that Potiphar bought Joseph for sexual purposes. However, when he tries to rape his slave, God hinders him. Joseph is saved and Potiphar is punished with castration. According to this interpretation, Potiphar is designated a "eunuch" in the text. Hebrew *saris*, however, which appears in Genesis 39 to describe Potiphar, can be translated either "eunuch" or as the title for a high-ranking officer in the royal administration (cf. Küchler 1986: 145–146).
13 The name "Mary" only applies to other women, never to Jesus's mother (cf. John 2:1–12, 19:25–27).

14 Concerning other texts (John 1:35–40; 18:15–6) mentioning an anonymous disciple, one can doubt if they refer to the same narrative figure as these disciples are not explicitly characterised by the love of Jesus (cf. John 13:23–25, 19:25–27, 20:2–10, 21:7, 20–24).

15 For biblical marital ideals cf. Ebach (2007: 179–180). For Greece and Rome, Glazebrook and Olson (2014) state: "Since the main goal of marriage was the production of legitimate heirs, sexual virtue was the most important quality for women and any female sexual activity outside of marriage was a sexual transgression. In contrast, men were not limited to their wives as sexual partners but could acceptably engage in sexual activity with their own slaves, commercial prostitutes, and citizen boys" (2014: 75).

16 If the text would want the reader to think of Joseph as being penetrated, or treated in any exceptional way by his master's wife, it would have been necessary in a patriarchal context to indicate this.

17 Therefore, we find only very few texts in the Hebrew Bible, where the beautiful man is the object of female desire without negative judgement (cf. for example Song 1:16, 5:10–16; 1 Samuel 18:20, 27–8 mention that Michal [king Saul's daughter] loves David, but her love is not connected with his beauty. On the topic of men's beauty, see the next chapter).

18 As marriage was based in most cases on a contract between a father and bridegroom, the consent of the bride was welcome but not necessary. The future husband had to convince more his intended father-in-law than his daughter. The father *gives* his daughter into marriage and the husband *takes* her. Even today the wedding ceremony shows the father (or someone representing him) guiding the bride to the altar, where the bridegroom is waiting to receive her.

19 The story defends patriarchal gender hierarchy and, therefore, does not intend to portray Joseph as a transgender-person, or as a "flaming young queen", as Carden (2006: 53) – based on Genesis 37 – puts it.

20 The gender hierarchy that the story presupposes is indicated clearly by the fact that the woman has nothing other to say than her sexual order (Gen 39:7, 10), while the man has a much longer and elaborate speech. As speaking is associated with power (in some texts, like Genesis 1:3, 6, 9, 11, 14, 20, 24, 26 and John 18:5–6, even with divine power) it is defined as masculine. Therefore, women are expected to be silent, while men should exert the power of the word (cf. Clines 1995: 217). Most patriarchal societies share this ideal (for Rome, cf. Deminion 2020).

21 See, however, the further development, as told in the following chapters: from Genesis 41:40 on, Joseph will rule over Egypt as viceroy of the Pharaoh.

Defending Masculinity Under Oppression 83

22 Such a construction of an extended public body of a master is not uncommon in slave-holder societies. See Proverbs 17:2. Some centuries later, the Roman philosopher Seneca will state that a slave acting in the name of the emperor can even be more powerful than a senator (cf. Seneca, Epistulae Morales 47,8–9).
23 For details of patriarchal marital laws cf. Ebach (2007: 179–180).
24 Even if the Persian time most probably is the era of origin for both the Holiness Code in Leviticus and the story in Genesis 39, one may ask if the portrayal of the strong woman who wants to share in the rights of her husband would not fit even better in Hellenistic times. Then, people throughout the Mediterranean world experienced upper-class women as ruling partners of their husbands. Especially the queens in Ptolemaic Egypt shared in the power of their husband-brothers and could even rule alone (after killing their brothers) if they decided to. Of course, this role model is not necessary for Potiphar's wife as the Egyptian housewife traditionally had a strong position and acted as "master of the house" (*nbt-pr*).
25 Gen 39 may even be seen as a narrative comment on what happens if fathers in "Israel" ignore Lev 18:21 and let their children pass to "Molech" (that is, the foreign king and his administration; cf. Hieke 2015: 35–36). Then "sons of Israel" might find themselves in the hands of foreign masters/rulers – with all the dangers given for their masculinity.

5 The Beautiful Ruler and the Ugly Redeemer

The previous chapter showed us a man who is beautiful in the eyes of a woman. Because this woman has power, she tries to victimise Joseph, the beautiful man. In the system of masculine domination her act violates the "proper" directionality of desire. As already mentioned above, biblical texts, inasmuch as they share in this cultural system, do not say much about women who are attracted to masculine beauty. The most prominent exception to this is the Song of Solomon (also known as the Song of Songs), a text which could even be understood as overcoming the patriarchal order of desire – at least on first view.

With the Eyes of a Woman? – Masculine Beauty in the Song of Solomon

The Song of Solomon celebrates erotic love without binding it to the uniting of families or securing of procreation. Love, with all its pleasures and pains, seems to be a value in and of itself, and any religious dimension to the gender relations is in the background – if indeed present at all. While date and place of origin are highly debated, it is obvious that this is a collection of love poetry, and its various parts most probably stem from different eras. While scholars deduce a pre-exilic date of origin for some parts, other parts indicate a post-exilic origin, and others may even point to a Hellenistic date of composition (cf. Hagedorn 2018).

The cultural context is possibly as diverse and multi-layered as the chronology. Similarity to Egyptian love poems is obvious;

additionally, Mesopotamian and Greek literature's influence is identifiable (cf. Exum 2005: 47–63). As to the social background, it is clear that a literary piece like the Song of Solomon presupposes a higher sociocultural echolon, even if popular traditions and motifs also find expression (cf. Exum 2005: 63).

Although it would be anachronistic to understand the Song of Solomon as a feminist text (cf. Clines 1995: 94–121; Exum 2005: 13–28; Tielesch 2013), the Song is striking insofar as it has a woman[1] praising the beauty of the beloved man (e.g. Song 1:16; 5:10–16). In spite of this prominence of a woman's voice, David Clines argues against female authorship, stating, the book "is a text written by an Israelite male to meet the desires and needs of other Israelite males" (1995: 99). Yet even if the text were to have been written by a woman (cf. Goitein 1993), she would have shared the norms and ideals of her culture to a certain extent. Anyway, the sex of the author(s) cannot be established and is less important for us than the gender perspective of the implied author, i.e. the intra-textual image given of the author. In relation to the latter, I follow Clines, who says that "the Song is the dream of a dream. The male author is dreaming a love poem, and the love poem takes the form of a woman's dream, of a woman dreaming her male lover's words" (1995: 104). I do not, however, accept his statement that the text wants "to repress the conflict of interests between the sexes by representing the female and male lovers as more or less equal, and their desire, capacities and satisfactions as more or less identical" (1995: 101). Sure, the social reality definitely was different from the imagined one, but the Song of Solomon should not be relegated to mere "pillow talk" (1995: 102). Rather, the Song creates a heterotopia, an ideal cultural space alternative to the strict gender order ruling ordinary life. Such alternative spaces do not immediately change reality but they open the mind of the reader to a world beyond the *status quo*. The "normal" world is not the only possible one. Therefore, heterotopic literature is not simply "escapist". Instead, texts like the Song of Songs bring with them the dangerous hope of unchaining the alternative world within the text and to let it loose in the life outside the text. Otherwise, it would not have been necessary for later reception to suppress the gender dynamics in the Song's celebration of human sexuality by resorting to allegorisation.[2]

As Simon Tielesch (2013: 59) states, the definition of masculine beauty uses patterns of masculine domination. The symbolism of the feminine gaze on the man's body (esp. in Song 5:10–16) supposes the association of masculine beauty with power, strength, and inviolability (cf. Tielesch 2013: 62). Thus, the Song of Solomon is no exception in linking the personal and the public body by orienting the ideal of masculine beauty towards establishing, securing, and exerting power. I would insist, however, on a specific change concerning the *function* of the beloved man's beauty. In the Song, masculine strength is celebrated exclusively because of its beauty. It is an aesthetic and erotic value not a practical one. The strength of the beloved is neither that of a worker, nor that of a warrior, or a rapist. It is seen as important to attract a woman but not as a means to labouring, conquering a city, defeating an enemy, or overpowering another human. In this point, the Song of Solomon is different from other biblical texts mentioning the beauty of a man.

The Hero's Power-Beauty

In cultural systems of masculine domination, the purpose of masculine beauty is not usually to attract the erotic interest of women. Instead, it serves communication between men. The beauty of a man is defined and acknowledged by other men. In biblical texts, this has little to do with homoerotic attraction – although such undertones cannot be dismissed completely. In the book of Daniel, the beauty of Judean young men plays a role when they are chosen to serve at the royal court of Babylon (Dan 1:4). In this case, one might assume that the service of these young courtiers might include sexual service for the king. But this possibility is never more than implied in the text. We cannot exclude the existence of silent cultural presuppositions in the text, but the beauty of the courtiers could also have no erotic overtones and be aimed at contributing to a beautiful ambience for the ruler. The same may be the case when the beauty of young David receives mention upon his selection for the service of King Saul (1 Sam 16:18).

The Beautiful Ruler and the Ugly Redeemer 87

While acknowledging the possibility, even regular occurrence, of a powerful man sexually abusing his male and female servants, one cannot say or assume that *every* ruler was applying his power in such a way or that every text mentioning beautiful servants insinuates or incites the imagination to picture such abuse. Insofar as royal courts were constructed as ideal spaces for a beautiful life, with commensurately beautiful architecture, interior decoration, clothing, food, fragrances, dancing, and music, good-looking servants fit well into this *Gesamtkunstwerk* (i.e. the totality of a work of art).[3]

The context in which biblical texts mention masculine beauty tends to indicate that power plays a major role. Most of the time it is powerful men, or men on their way to power, or aspiring to power, who are characterised as beautiful. Saul, David (1 Sam 16:12,18; 17:42), Absalom (2 Sam 14:25), and, in more general terms, the king (Ps 45:3; Isa 33:17) are all men who are called beautiful. Most probably, the tight link between masculine beauty, physical strength, and heroic power is an archaic one, dating from times when a man's leadership was primarily based on his body-size and physical strength. Of course, in a developed state like Egypt, it is the royal administration (i.e. the king's extended body), which exerts the king's power. Yet, the symbolic value of physical strength never got lost out of sight. Even in the New Kingdom and later, a ruler had to show his bodily fitness for ruling by celebrating the Sed festival, which included (at least virtually) several sporting exercises (see Figure 5.1).

The tradition of beauty signifying vitality and strength can be found in 1 Samuel 9:2, where the supreme beauty of Saul, the future king, is exemplified in him being taller than all others. Here, the text clearly connects royal power, beauty, and physical strength. This archaic association is much less pronounced in the biblical references to David's beauty.

Strikingly, David's elder brothers are taller and stronger than he is. God, however, ignores them and choses the youngest, who is probably, in contrast to Saul, shortest. Nevertheless, David is called beautiful (1 Sam 16:12). Obviously, his beauty does not here signify body-strength. Some verses on (1 Sam 16:18), the narrator links David's beauty with the power of a courageous

88 The Beautiful Ruler and the Ugly Redeemer

Figure 5.1 Relief at Karnak[4]

warrior and with musical abilities.[5] Yet, even the warrior qualities are not necessarily associated physical strength, otherwise there would be no reason for the giant Goliath to disdain him as young, ruddy, and beautiful (1 Sam 17:42). David achieves his victory over Goliath's massive body-strength by using a simple weapon in an intelligent way (1 Sam 17:49–50).[6] Obviously, his heroic beauty consists in other qualities than mere body-size. Beside the fact of generally looking good, his beautiful eyes (1 Sam 16:12) and his "ruddiness"[7] (16:12; 17:42) receive mention. These characteristics do not disqualify David from meeting the ideal of aggressive masculinity. Clines ascertains the victims of David as "something like 140,000 men, in addition to the

15 individuals whose deaths he is said to have been personally responsible for" (1995: 217). This king is a killer.

David's sexual conduct, meanwhile, presupposes the principal norm of rape culture: "Take what you can!" The Bathsheba episode (2 Sam 11) is the key example. David, as he emerges from the narration, is not involved in deep emotions towards his at least 18 wives. Even in the case of Bathsheba "the sex is essentially an expression of royal power, and it is much more like rape than love" (Clines 1995: 226). There is no mention of Bathsheba's perspective and certainly not of any attraction on her part to David's looks. David's beauty plays no role in the depictions of his relationships with women, not even when the text mentions Michal's love for David (1 Sam 18:20, 27–28).

In the story of Absalom, the rebellious prince, beauty, body-strength and (royal) power unravel in a specific way. His beauty consists in a completely flawless body (2 Sam 14:25) and an enormous head of hair (14:26). Even if plenty of long hair can be associated with virility[8] or with preparedness for war (Ackerman 1998: 32–33), in Absalom's case, it does not convey the masculinity of a successful fighter, as the brutal and shameful end of this beautiful man teaches the reader (2 Sam 18:9–15).[9] Reading back the Absalom story, his beauty is a dysfunctional one, the beauty of a man who wants to be king but fails. Here, not even rape (2 Sam 16:21–23) can enhance his masculinity enough. Although Absalom "has sex with ten of his father's secondary wives 'in the sight of all Israel' simply in order to lay claim to the throne of his father" (Clines 1995: 226),[10] he proves himself incapable of becoming king. Although the Absalom episode attributes beauty to a man who fails in being a ruler, it does not loosen the tight link between masculine beauty and power. It just says that the masculine beauty has to be the right one.

The Beauty of the Anointed King: Reflection of God's Power

While only a small number of named kings are called beautiful in the Hebrew Bible, the programmatic character of the association between masculine beauty and power can be seen clearly in Psalm 45 and its depiction of the ideal king.

Some parts (e.g. Ps 45:2–10, 17–18) may date back to pre-exilic times, reflecting early royal ideology (cf. Zenger & Hossfeld 1993: 279; sceptical on that is Böhler 2021: 821). But, for our purposes, chronology is not decisive. Psalm 45 praises kingship, not any specific king. Therefore, the song can refer to a post-exilic wish-king as well as to any pre-exilic ruler who claimed to fulfil the requirements of ideal kingship. Verses 3–9 create a blueprint of true kingship that links supreme beauty with martial qualities as well as with religious and social values:

> [3] You are beautiful more than (all) the sons of Adam,
> And grace has been poured upon your lips,
> Therefore, God has blessed you forever.
> [4] Gird your sword on the hip, you hero: your glory and your majesty.
> [5] Your majesty (may) ride on victoriously on behalf of truth and humility and justice;
> Let your right hand teach you terrifying things.
> [6] Your arrows are sharpened – peoples will fall under you – in the heart of the king's enemies.
> [7] Your throne, o god[11], is forever and ever,
> A sceptre of righteousness is the sceptre of your kingdom.
> [8] You love justice and hate lawlessness,
> Therefore, your God has anointed you, o god, with the oil of joy more than your fellows.
> [9] Myrrh and aloes, (and) cassia (in) all your garments,
> From ivory palaces, string-music delights you.

The most beautiful man, chosen, blessed, and anointed by God, administers a kingdom of grace, glory, justice, and righteousness, a kingdom that establishes a world order according to God's will. The king's supreme beauty, as well as the fragrances that surround him being in his garment (or even being his garment?), are indicators of his close relationship with God (cf. Bechmann 2000: 93–94) who installed him as king. This relationship is so close that the song even addresses the perfect king himself as *elohim* (god): that is, using the same term regularly used as an address for the deity (translated "God"). This is not a personal deification but a descriptor of the royal office, similar to the title n_tr nfr (visible/perfect god) used for the Egyptian king.[12] The king's reign in both instances comes *from* God, his power is given *by* God, God is reigning *through* him, and so the king is, effectively, a god. By virtue of his office, the god-king is the representative of God, a kind of living sacrament for God's active presence (cf. Zenger & Hossfeld 1993: 279–282).

In Psalm 45 masculine beauty is clearly linked with power. This is the beauty of a royal ruler. Although his kingship aims at justice and righteousness, it is not free from violence. Sword, riding on a horse (or on a war-chariot), and sharp arrows are mentioned. Terror is involved and enemies must fall. The beautiful god-king is a fighter. The social values (truth, humility, righteousness, and justice) he is standing for must be enacted with power and violence. Even if all the military terms are only metaphors, it is significant that the imagery of war and battle is used to signify the god-king.[13] According to the psalm, even the noblest social values need power and violence for their implementation, and the strong ruler as God's tool achieves such. Therefore, in Psalm 45, too, masculine beauty is not just an aesthetic category; it is one element in a set of characteristics qualifying a ruler and fighter. His ultimate intentions may seem desirable and to suggest stability and peace but his methods are within the framework of masculine domination. Although the song mentions penetrating weapons, one can be happy that at least violent sexuality plays no role here in the portrait of the ideal king. One might ask, however, if the women "given" to this king have a choice in the matter; they certainly have no voice (cf. Ps 45:10–16).

The Ugly Redeemer

The image of a man dying on the cross is the image of a victim, helpless, humiliated, and suffering, an ugly image in painful contrast to the image of the beautiful, mighty king. Although Christian readers are accustomed to the New Testament's interpretation of Jesus as a king, following the traditions of the Hebrew Bible and of early Jewish messianism, one should realise that this dual image is discordant. Even Paul, the most important preacher of the crucified Jesus, acknowledges that talking about a messiah-king on the cross is not very plausible (cf. 1 Cor 1:17,23).

After all, Paul knew very well that crucifixion was the ugliest and most shameful death penalty of his time. Crucifixion[14] was regarded as so shameful and dishonouring that it was not used to punish Roman citizens but, more typically, persons of low status, like slaves, and non-Romans, such as inhabitants of occupied territories – most often rebels against the Roman order (*pax romana*), those designated terrorists and other ignominious outlaws. This method of execution signifies the intention to kill not only the personal body but also to destroy the public body of the delinquent. Crucifixion was so terrifying that Cicero writes one should not even mention the word "cross" in front of a Roman citizen (Cicero, Pro Rabirio 5,16). The Jewish historiographer Josephus Flavius mentions crucifixion as the "most miserable death" (Josephus, Bellum Iudaicum 7,203). Crucifixion entailed a string of horrors and the intended terror was effected by several means:

- *Torture*: The victim lacked any human right and experienced profound physical pain and indignity, not only on the cross itself, but even prior, such as flagellation, other forms of beating, and sexual abuse.
- *Forced nakedness*: The person had to suffer and to die naked in a public place.[15]
- *Display*: The cross functioned as a site of exhibition, showing the naked, helpless, and suffering person to the public. Although, it was an exception to use very high crosses, a delinquent was publicly exposed.
- *Duration*: Depending on the physical constitution of the person, dying on the cross could take several hours, or even days.
- *Decay*: In most cases, the corpse of the victim was not buried in an individual grave to avoid any after-life in the memory of family and friends. Corpses were sometimes left at the cross to decay before the eyes of the public. If a burial was granted, in most cases a mass grave close to the execution place was used.

The listed horrors were part of a political communication between rulers and subordinates. Crucifixion was not only excruciating and horrendous for the victim; it was also intended as a deterrent, to instil terror in those who witnessed it. Each of the listed elements was open to casual variations, because crucifixion was a punishment beyond law. Although it was practised by state authorities, there were no regulations on how to do it exactly. Only Roman citizens were protected by specific rights but usually they were not sentenced to crucifixion. The typical victims of crucifixion are non-Romans without any civil rights. Therefore, there was no limit or restriction on cruel fantasy on the part of executioners.

In early Judaism, the reference to Deuteronomy 21:23 ("any hanged one is a curse of God") played an additional role in understanding crucifixion. Although Deuteronomy 21:22–23 did not originally refer to crucifixion, but was a regulation that limited the shameful display of the corpse of any dead person,[16] it went on to be read as a negative judgement on the victims of crucifixion in the Roman era. Therefore, it is understandable that in the Jewish context, the cross never became a positive symbol of heroic death or martyrdom although many religiously motivated Jewish rebels died on the cross.

Under the aspect of gender, crucifixion is a man's ultimate de-masculinisation. Because the cultural framework of masculine domination combines power, beauty, glory, honour, masculinity, and god, the ruler representing god on earth is the most masculine person,[17] while the crucified Jesus appears as helpless, ugly, humiliated, godforsaken, and therefore as deprived of masculinity. Therefore, the crucified man is, on a symbolic level, equivalent with the sexually penetrated man, no matter whether the humiliating initial tortures leading up to crucifixion entailed or implied sexual abuse or not. It is also not decisive whether the body of the crucified victim was fixed to the cross with nails or penetrated in another way.[18] Whatever the case, the crucified man, like the sexually penetrated man, experiences feminisation, because crucifixion signifies, even displays, the annihilation of masculinity.

As the addressees of early Christian preaching could, under certain circumstances, still experience crucifixion as eyewitnesses, they must have been very sensitive to the paradox of calling a crucified man "son of god". Therefore, one must ask how at all, such a paradoxical message could gain any plausibility. I see two possible answers. The first pertains to the belief in Jesus's resurrection, and the second to the Hebrew Bible's tradition of the suffering servant of God. The latter idea, of a suffering man in a redemptive role, is developed in the book of Isaiah. Here the anonymous servant or slave of God, depicted in Isaiah 53, is a redeemer who is ugly, without any masculine beauty or glory (Isa 53:2). While being disdained and rejected, he assumes the diseases, pain, misdeeds, and sin of others and even gives his life for them (53:3–5,12). The servant's vicarious death has a redemptive effect; his death functions as an offering and achieves atonement (53:10). He is in the role of the sacrificial animal and not in that of the king or priest making the offering.

The ugly image of a pierced (53:5) and crushed (53:10) slave is exactly the opposite of the glorious image of a ruler cloaked in masculine beauty, glory, and power, which we saw in Psalm 45. Given Jesus's mortal life ended on the cross, early Christians felt invited to identify him with the servant of God in the book of Isaiah, especially as this allowed for the attribution of a salvific meaning to his suffering and death. Jesus in the role of the slave, giving his life for others, can be found, for instance, in Mark 10:45 and in the Last Supper tradition (Mark 14:24), where it is combined with the idea of a (new) covenant (deriving mainly from the book of Jeremiah but also found in Isaiah 54:10 and 55:3). Additionally, Acts 8:27–35 mentions the evangelist Philip preaching the gospel of Jesus based on Isaiah 53:7–8.[19]

However, the identification of Jesus with Isaiah's servant of God was only plausible *after* the Jesus-movement was convinced that their master was the messiah: that is, following the visionary experiences of Jesus's resurrection and exaltation (cf. 1 Cor 15:5–8). Given this conviction, the identification with the servant became even more inviting, as Isaiah 53 talks not only about vicarious suffering but also about new life as the reward for the self-sacrificing slave (53:10–12).

Jesus Christ Passing Through Genders

Just as in the case of Deutero-Isaiah's servant of God, the post-Easter theology understood Jesus's resurrection and exaltation as a divine confirmation of his mission and message. The original message of resurrection was not about returning into earthly life. Instead, we can learn from the tradition that Paul quotes in his letters that resurrection and exaltation were seen as the same. Instead of remaining in *sheol*, the usual shadowy underworld abode of the deceased, Jesus is elevated to heaven, installed as messianic king, and granted the status of God's son. This message is exactly what Paul, relying on older tradition, expresses in Romans 1:4, where he says that Jesus was "defined as Son of God in power according to the Spirit of holiness out of the resurrection from the dead".[20]

The belief that God acknowledges Jesus as his son by resurrecting and enthroning him made it possible to reinterpret the shameful death on the cross by attributing a salvific purpose to it. The curse of the cross turns into blessing. And because the gender symbolism of masculine domination associates humiliation and shame with feminisation, the reinterpretation of the cross in positive terms produces a gender paradox. The glory of God (i.e. the highest masculinity) displays in something feminine. The gender drama implied in the dialectic of early Christian soteriology, therefore, can be understood as a trans-gender journey.

This applies first, to the historical Jesus: as a lower-class Jew form a tiny and unimportant village belonging to an occupied territory, Jesus was a person without political rights. Thus, his political body does not show much masculinity. Even his sociocultural body is not very masculine, as he is uneducated[21] and apparently living without wife and children – as far as we tell from the gospels. Of course, his teaching and healing are masculine traits in the cultural framework of the time. However, crucifixion destroys all masculinity of Jesus's public body. This ultimate feminisation is "repaired" by the belief in his resurrection as an exaltation to divine masculinity. The public body of a son of God, sitting (or standing) side by side with God (cf. Hengel 1993; Kügler 2011: 338–339) in heavenly glory, is one of ultimate masculinity, according to the gender code of ancient culture.

Secondly, the passage through genders is even more dramatic in the framework of pre-existence Christology, which lets the journey start in heaven, sees a divine person come down on earth, and then return to God. This Christological pattern, most probably derived from Jewish wisdom-theology, is a quite old element of early Christian theology, as can be seen in Philippians 2:6–11. There, Paul quotes a pre-Pauline hymn describing the circular movement "heaven-earth-heaven" that at the same time is a journey through different genders and statuses:

Text of the Hymn	*Power/Status*	**Gender** aspect
⁶ ὃς ἐν μορφῇ θεοῦ ὑπάρχων οὐχ ἁρπαγμὸν ἡγήσατο τὸ εἶναι ἴσα θεῷ, Being in god-form, he did not interpret being god-like as (his) private portion,	Divine status	Divine masculinity
⁷ ἀλλ' ἑαυτὸν ἐκένωσεν μορφὴν δούλου λαβών, ἐν ὁμοιώματι ἀνθρώπων γενόμενος· καὶ σχήματι εὑρεθεὶς ὡς ἄνθρωπος Rather, he emptied himself, adopting slave-form, born in human likeness and found like human in appearance, ⁸ ἐταπείνωσεν ἑαυτὸν γενόμενος ὑπήκοος μέχρι θανάτου, θανάτου δὲ σταυροῦ. he humbled himself, being obedient unto death – death even of (the) cross.	Renunciation of power Subordination Humiliation Obedience Loss of self-determination Death Social annihilation (cross)	Gradual de-masculinisation into complete feminisation (crucifixion)
⁹ διὸ καὶ ὁ θεὸς αὐτὸν ὑπερύψωσεν καὶ ἐχαρίσατο αὐτῷ τὸ ὄνομα τὸ ὑπὲρ πᾶν ὄνομα,	Exaltation Divine highness Most powerful name	Ultimate divine masculinity

(Continued)

Text of the Hymn	Power/Status	Gender aspect
Therefore, God exalted him and granted him the name above every name, [10] ἵνα ἐν τῷ ὀνόματι Ἰησοῦ πᾶν γόνυ κάμψῃ ἐπουρανίων καὶ ἐπιγείων καὶ καταχθονίων so that in the name of Jesus every knee may bow, of the heavenly, eartly and underworldly ones [11] καὶ πᾶσα γλῶσσα ἐξομολογήσηται ὅτι κύριος Ἰησοῦς Χριστὸς εἰς δόξαν θεοῦ πατρός. and every tongue may confess: Lord (is) Jesus Christ to the glory of God the father!	Universal reign Acknowledged Lord over heaven, earth, and underworld	

According to the binary gender logic of antiquity, the gradual loss of masculinity implies a gradual feminisation of the public body. The cross marks the total loss of masculinity, i.e. complete feminisation. Being exalted by God to universal glory and power, in contrast, implies perfect masculinity. Philippians 2:6–11 does not see the status of exaltation as a mere restitution of the heavenly status prior to "adopting slave-form". Instead, the new status is associated with honours that were not mentioned before. Most probably, this has to do with the difference in audience. The first god-like status supposes no interaction with any public ("private portion", 2:6), and this is the reason for leaving it behind: Christ does not consider it as his "private portion" (2:6). For him, the divine status needs communication and sharing, which he achieves by giving up divinity in submitting to humiliation and death. Therefore, the finally achieved status is greater than the first one. Now, a universal public acknowledges the masculine power and glory of Jesus's public body: heavenly, earthly, and underworldly beings all submit to his reign – a greater public than this cosmic one is not possible. Of course,

Christ's gender journey implies the personal body of Jesus as well; born into his personal body, he suffers and dies. However, only the public body is of religious importance. The public body starts in divine masculinity, suffers feminisation, and achieves greatest divine masculinity in the end.

Relevant Insights for Recent Debate?

Jesus's experience of being de-masculinised in suffering and crucifixion is an important aspect of Christian spirituality. And yet, it is an ambivalent one. In the Middle Ages, many spiritual authors and artists interpreted Christ as mother of the faithful. The mystical Mother Christ gives birth to the Church through the side-wound (mentioned in John 19:34: "one of the soldiers with a spear pierced his side") and nourishes children with their own blood.[22] But such veneration of Jesus as a transgender mother did not break up the system of masculine domination as the general guideline for practice in church and state. Neither did transgender, or gender-ambiguous persons find much acceptance in Christian society, nor were women admitted to leading roles. Although women were embraced as virgin saints, leaders of monasteries, mystical authors, and more, their exclusion from ordination to the roles of priests and bishops persisted. Instead of ordaining women or transgender persons to represent Christ as mother, the leading men in church were invited to develop a spirituality of maternity. Theologians like the crusade-preacher Bernard of Clairvaux tried to integrate the femininity of Christ into masculine church-power (cf. Angenendt 1997: 141–143). Thus, the male church-leader should function as father *and* mother on a spiritual *and* pastoral level. Although being only a man on the level of the personal body, the ideal church-leader becomes the complete human person by developing a religious body that unites femininity and masculinity. Therefore, the leading churchman is capable of representing the masculine, as well as the feminine, aspects of Christ: consequently, there is no need for women. This historical experience with the veneration of Jesus as a bi-gendered redeemer should inform modern discussions on gender equality and non-gendered structures

The Beautiful Ruler and the Ugly Redeemer 99

in religious (and other) communities, because the link between theory and practice is important. Obviously, it is not enough to venerate the redeemer as a motherly man (or Mary as a powerful virgin-mother). Two questions are crucial: first, who is entitled to represent these religious authorities on earth? And second, what is the role of the personal body's gender in this representation?

Additionally, the tradition of the victimised redeemer plays an important role in recent discussion on sexual abuse in the Catholic Church and other religious settings.[23] Of course, it is inviting for innocent victims of sexual abuse to identify spiritually with Jesus, another innocent victim (cf. Figueroa & Tombs 2020). If survivors experience healing in doing so, nobody ought to criticise that. However, one should not ignore the implied risks. As Christian theology attributes a redemptive function to Jesus's suffering and death, the spiritual identification with Jesus can result in a glorification of suffering as a way to heaven. Using this concept as a pastoral technique for comforting survivors of abuse certainly could have a re-traumatising effect rather than a healing one. It might even contribute to exculpating, or exonerating, perpetrators and their supporters. Therefore, it is a first step to challenging the traditional theology of atonement as Heath (2011: 123–132) and others already have (cf. Reaves & Tombs 2019: 402–404). Yet, it is necessary to stress the contextual character of religious truth and theological expression. To identify Jesus as a victim of sexual violence has a different meaning for survivors, for perpetrators, and for witnesses/observers.

- For *survivors*, identifying with Jesus as abused can have a healing function, as already mentioned above.
- Identifying the victims with Jesus may also imply an important message for *perpetrators*. Even if they are churchmen, they are not allowed to identify with Jesus, as this role goes to their victims. Therefore, abusers have to identify with those who were abusing Jesus. Being identified as enemies of Christ certainly is a painful experience but it can also be a cathartic clarification that can be healing if it leads to acknowledgement of guilt and repentance.

- Again, identification of victims with Jesus can make sense of any *persons aware of abuse*. If the victims are representing Jesus, ignoring the suffering of victims, contributing in their stigma, blaming the victims, or exculpating abusers is no option.

Thus, the identification of victims can initiate a role-play with effects of healing and even prevention. However, the exclusion of any cynical glorification of suffering is indispensable.[24]

Notes

1 It is important to add that the text does not describe or gender the speakers (only the addressee is). However, it is plausible to assume a woman-man dialogue and love-match.
2 On the development of allegorical interpretation, see, for example, Clines (1995: 110–114) and Exum (2005: 73–77).
3 Not only the temple (cf. Smoak 2021) as the residence of God, but also the king's residence could be seen as an image of the perfect world. Therefore, temple and palace have similar decorations and are often mentioned together. On the beauty of Solomon's palace, cf. 1 Kings 7:1–12; 10:4–22 (cf. also Ps 45:9).
4 Simplified graphic adapted from https://commons.wikimedia.org/wiki/File:Thutmosis-sedfestlauf.jpg (accessed 13/04/2022) and created by the author. On the Sed ritual, cf. Shaw and Nicholson (2008: 287–288); Hornung and Staehelin (2006).
5 On music under the aspect of masculinity, cf. Clines (1995: 227–228).
6 In a way that is pretty sexualised, too. As Stephen Wilson points out the text characterises "Goliath as a feminized sexual victim of the newly minted man, David" (2015: 101).
7 It is not clear what "ruddy" means. One might think of fair or reddish skin and/or hair – something exceptional in the ancient Near East.
8 Silvia Schroer (1992: 176) refers to the example of Samson in Judges 16. However, Samson is not called beautiful.
9 This is even truer when the end of Absalom is associated with his long hair, as the history of reception usually does (cf. Schroer 1992: 181).
10 Cynthia Chapman (2004: 35) refers to Assyrian inscriptions seeing a defeated king's harem as spoil.
11 Although Hebrew has no capital or lower case letter distinction, my translation uses "god" when I understand the text as referring to the king, while I use "God" when I think the text is referring to YHWH.

12 Obviously, even today dogmatic ideas hinder commentators to translate *'elohim* properly (cf. Böhler's [2021: 817–818] problems). If *'elohim* is used for Moses in relation to Aaron (Ex 4:16) and Pharaoh (Ex 7:1), and even for the spirit of a dead (1 Sam 28:13), what can be so exceptional in using it for the divine king? It is time to accept that the term *'elohim* not always means the one and only God, but also "second-class" entities of considerable or superhuman power.

13 On God and his agents as warriors cf. Ryan (2019) and Thiede (2022: 78–98).

14 For more details of practice and meaning of crucifixion, cf. Kügler (2011: 331–337); Cook (2014); Tombs (2017).

15 In antiquity (as in most cultures), the symbolic value of nakedness depends on the context. It can be an expression of leisure and wellness in the public baths or show supreme power (like in the cases of naked gods and heroes). However, forced nakedness clearly is a sign of humiliation (cf. Heath 2011: 123; Greenough 2021: 62–64).

16 On the stigma of exposed corpses, see the humiliating display of Saul's corpse (1 Sam 31:10), or Rizpah protecting the corpses of her sons until they were granted burial (2 Sam 21:9–14), and the displaying of Holofernes's head (Judith 12:12–16).

17 The statue "Augustus of Prima Porta" (marble, 1st-century CE, Vatican Museums, Inv. 2290) represents this ideal of masculinity. For a picture see: www.museivaticani.va/content/museivaticani/de/collezioni/musei/braccio-nuovo/Augusto-di-Prima-Porta.html (accessed 13/04/2022). For the classical Greek idea of masculine beauty, see e.g. the "Riace Warriors" (https://scholarexchange.furman.edu/art231/40/ [accessed 13/04/2022]) or the Roman copy of Polycleitus's bronze statue of a spear-fighter "doryphoros" (Inv. 6011) at the Museo Archeologico Nazionale of Naples (https://commons.wikimedia.org/wiki/File:Doryphoros_MAN_Napoli_Inv6011-2.jpg [accessed 13/04/2022]).

18 Tombs (2017: 105–106) refers to ancient sources mentioning special constructions that made the crucified victim suffer anal penetration. Cf. Max Klinger's painting "Kreuzigung Christi" (1890) for a visual representation of this topic (https://digiboard5.htwk-leipzig.de/ausstellung/unterhaltung/kunstausstellung/max-klinger/ [accessed 13/04/2022]).

19 On the reception history of Isaiah 53, cf. Goldingay and Payne (2006: 284–288).

20 Cf. the same concept in Acts 13:33 (cf. Kügler 1997: 318–320).

21 According to the elite standards of the time, Aramaic-speaking Jesus was a *barbaros*, a person lacking Hellenistic-Roman education.

22 John 19:34 mentions also blood and water coming out from the spear-wound. Middle Ages exegesis understood these elements as

referring to the sacraments of the Church (eucharist and baptism) and declared the Church herself to be born out of Jesus's wound as his motherly womb. As Jesus nourishes the faithful with his blood (as Eucharistic wine) the side-wound functioned also as a maternal breast (cf. Bynum 1992: 99–211).

23 For the debate, cf. Tombs (1999), Heath (2011), Trainor (2014), Reaves and Tombs (2019), Kügler (2020), Greenough (2021: 62–82), and many more.

24 In Germany, Catholic Bishops Voderholzer and Overbeck recently had a fierce debate on whether victims of abuse are infallible teachers of faith (cf. https://www.feinschwarz.net/verachtung-vom-unfehlbaren-lehramt-der-betroffenen/ [accessed 13/04/2022]). Voderholzer tries to avoid structural changes in the Church and, therefore, refuses using this dogmatic category. His opponent Overbeck holds that identifying the victims with Jesus inevitably grants them this authority. Theologically, Overbeck's conclusion is inescapable. If Christians identify survivors with Jesus, they owe victims' testimony comparable faith and trust as Jesus's testimony.

6 "God-Wives", "Old Virgins", "Young Widows"

Women Without Human Husbands

In many ancient languages, the words translating "widow" refer not only to a once married woman whose husband died. Instead, Hebrew *'almanah*, Greek *chera*, and Latin *vidua* all pertain to a woman without a man in a very general way (cf. Beck 2020: 17). Such "a woman without a man" is not simply an unmarried woman but someone with no male lord at all: neither a father, nor brothers, neither a husband, nor slaveholder, nor any other male relative, is responsible for her. A woman without a man might today be called free and independent but in ancient societies, her status would be construed not as *free from* but as *lacking* masculine domination. This is so because in patriarchal cultures masculine domination of women is constructed in part as an act of responsibility, protection, and guidance, not (ostensibly) as suppression and exploitation.[1] A woman without a lord was, in effect, a non-person and very socially vulnerable, not least because the usual associations a woman had within the social realm were mediated through her male patron(s) who acted as an anchor with the world outside the house (cf. Beck 2020: 17–67). Therefore, it was not desirable for women to be "free from" masculine domination. In ancient Egypt, as well as in the implied social contexts of the Hebrew Bible, the widow – together with the orphan, the stranger, and the sick – is paradigmatic of the poor and helpless. On this account, they were attributed as having a special relationship to the deity. In the Bible, many texts[2] see YHWH as the friend and helper of widows, defending social justice on their behalf, as well as on that of other destitute groups

DOI: 10.4324/9781003269977-7

(cf. Kügler 2017: 216–219). In Egypt, Amun can even function as the "husband" of the widows and as the "father and mother" of the helpless (cf. Kügler 2017: 218–219).

However, the situation of women in the absence of a masculine patron being helpless, and without rights or power, was not automatic, or without exception. There are some few examples of women's singlehood where not (ever) having a human husband, or other male protector, transpires in elevated status and some – sometimes considerable – power.

The Egyptian Institution of "God's Wife of Amun"

In his "Histories", the Greek author Herodotus (5th-century BCE) mentions a woman who sleeps with Amun-Zeus in his temple at Thebes, while renouncing any mortal men (Histories II, 182). Most probably, this refers to the royal priestess of Amun, a religious office of considerable political importance for the region of Thebais in Upper Egypt. Since 1070 BCE, this region was semi-independent from the king in the North and declared itself a theocracy ruled directly by Amun. In modern terms, one could perhaps call it a dictatorship of the high priest of Amun but officially, the ruler was Amun. The god spoke through his high priest as well as through his wife on earth, the aforementioned priestess who held the title "God's wife of Amun" (ḥm.t nṯr n.t 'Imn).[3] Often, the priestess was a daughter of the king in the North, while the high priest was drawn from the priestly aristocracy of the South (cf. Ayad 2016: 97–99). Therefore, the God's wife linked Thebais with the northern kingdom and functioned as a counterweight to the power ambitions of the local priesthood. Some of the God's wives achieved political power higher than that of the high priest; sometimes the office of the high priest was disempowered, or even kept vacant, subsumed into the role of God's wife. In such cases, God's wife of Amun was the *de facto* ruler of Upper Egypt.

A prominent example of such a powerful ruler is God's wife Shepenupet I (23rd Dynasty). The decoration of her Osiris-chapel at Karnak attributes royal qualities to her.

The original façade of the chapel "was dominated by scenes showing Shepenupet shaking the sistrum before Amun, Re-Horakhty, and Ptah, suckled[4] by Hathor and Semat-Weret, and crowned by Amun" (Ayad 2009b: 37). Shepenupet I's Nubian successor Amenirdi, who stressed continuity with her predecessor, stated her direct descent from Osiris and claimed the royal privilege of receiving the symbol of the Sed-festival (see above, Chapter 5). Her "investiture coincided with a gap of 50 years during which the office of High Priest of Amun was left vacant" (Ayad 2009b: 49).

Although God's wife of Amun plays a religio-political role similar to that of the king, no masculinisation of her public body takes place, as it did with Hatshepsut. Instead, the religio-political body is clearly feminine as the legitimation of power derives from Amun as her divine husband. Because this husband is absent, his wife represents him on earth. The royal father-son relationship is substituted by a husband-wife relationship. This transformation requires a "monogamous" life on the part of Amun's wife. Egyptian tradition knew polygamy only in the case of the king, while for any other man or woman monogamy was the common form of marriage. As for God's wife of Amun, any additional, earthly husband had to be excluded, as such a husband might have dominated his wife and threatened the balance of power between North and South by begetting children and creating a new dynasty, competing with the existing royal line. Therefore, "monogamy" in this case means the same as "celibacy"[5]: an earthly, human husband was impossible and sexual intercourse with a deity is an idea, not a bodily reality. Therefore, women holding the office of Amun's wife are part of the history of women who gain power by renouncing marriage and children, even if they were not regarded as "single women", "virgins", or "widows".

Rich, Beautiful, and Empowered by God: Judith

The biblical[6] book of Judith, written towards the end of the 2nd-century BCE (cf. Schmitz & Engel 2014: 61–63), reflects how in Hellenistic time the status of some single women changed (see above, Chapter 2). Instead of being poor, helpless, and marginalised, Judith is depicted as a widow, who is beautiful, rich, independent, and highly esteemed in her society. After the death of her husband Manasseh, she stays unmarried. Inheriting Manasseh's property, she lives as the non-working[7] head of a great household.

καὶ ἦν καλὴ τῷ εἴδει καὶ ὡραία τῇ ὄψει σφόδρα
And she was of beautiful look and of exceedingly lovely appearance,
καὶ ὑπελίπετο αὐτῇ Μανασσης ὁ ἀνὴρ αὐτῆς χρυσίον καὶ ἀργύριον καὶ παῖδας καὶ παιδίσκας καὶ κτήνη καὶ ἀγρούς
and her man Manasseh had left her gold and silver, and boy-servants and maid-servants, and cattle and fields,
καὶ ἔμενεν ἐπ' αὐτῶν
and she stayed upon them.

(Judith 8:7)

The text does not say why she was entitled to inherit from her husband and keep the property under her control, but maybe a lack of male relatives allowed her to do so. Anyway, the text communicates no necessity to give a reason for her right to inherit. This reflects changes in Hellenistic time that gave more opportunities of independence to women. We may also ask, what is the purpose of stressing Judith's beauty in connection with her role as the head of such a wealthy household? Is this a feminine analogy to masculine power-beauty? I think, a bit later the text gives an answer.

Judith can afford to spend her time with praying and fasting, and she has a special relationship to God. This relationship is a heritage of the traditional widow concept of the Hebrew Bible. It appears also when Judith stresses her "poverty" and "weakness" urging God to act as her helper (Judith 9:11) in killing the aggressor. The social need of the traditional widow is now transformed into a spiritual one; "poverty" no longer refers to a precarious economic situation but to need of the Almighty's help. The ascetic religious life of Judith not only qualifies her for her special deed, it is also a means of social control over her sexuality. She lives in a tent on top of her house, i.e. in a semi-public area.[8] Everybody can know that she is keeping away from men. Judith 8:8 states accordingly:

καὶ οὐκ ἦν ὃς ἐπήνεγκεν αὐτῇ ῥῆμα πονηρόν ὅτι ἐφοβεῖτο τὸν θεὸν σφόδρα
And there was no one who brought up a bad word about her because she feared God exceedingly.

Her piety and sexual abstinence are important characteristics. Together with her wealth, beauty, and prestige in society, these aspects create the image of a woman who deliberately renounces marriage. Judith 16:22 explicitly states:

καὶ πολλοὶ ἐπεθύμησαν αὐτήν καὶ οὐκ ἔγνω ἀνὴρ αὐτὴν πάσας τὰς ἡμέρας τῆς ζωῆς αὐτῆς ἀφ' ἧς ἡμέρας ἀπέθανεν Μανασσης ὁ ἀνὴρ αὐτῆς καὶ προσετέθη πρὸς τὸν λαὸν αὐτοῦ
And many desired her and (= but) no man knew
(= had sex with) her all the days of her life since the days that Manasseh her man died and was laid with his people (= buried).

Judith's sexual renunciation harmonises her personal body with her public body. Economic independence, public speech of wisdom,[9] and social prestige masculinise her public body; and she masculinises her personal body by not allowing any man to dominate her sexually. In the text, this double masculinity is the precondition for her public role as saviour. Like a king, she becomes the tool of God in redeeming his people from Assyrian aggression. Although the saving role is traditionally a masculine role attributed to the king, a widow can also play it if this is God's will. Using a "female hand" (Judith 9:10) to defeat his enemies glorifies God's omnipotence even more. The brave act of killing Holofernes, of course, highlights Judith's masculinity, especially as she uses a sword, the phallic weapon of masculine domination. At the same time, the way in which she gets access to her victim highlights her femininity.

> καὶ περιείλατο τὸν σάκκον ὃν ἐνεδεδύκει καὶ ἐξεδύσατο τὰ ἱμάτια τῆς χηρεύσεως αὐτῆς
> ³ And she took off the sackcloth that she was wearing and put aside the garment of her widowhood
> καὶ περιεκλύσατο τὸ σῶμα ὕδατι καὶ ἐχρίσατο μύρῳ παχεῖ καὶ διέξανε τὰς τρίχας τῆς κεφαλῆς αὐτῆς καὶ ἐπέθετο μίτραν ἐπ' αὐτῆς
> and she washed the body with water and anointed it with creamy perfume and she combed the hair of her head and put a head-band on it
> καὶ ἐνεδύσατο τὰ ἱμάτια τῆς εὐφροσύνης αὐτῆς ἐν οἷς ἐστολίζετο ἐν ταῖς ἡμέραις τῆς ζωῆς τοῦ ἀνδρὸς αὐτῆς Μανασση
> and she dressed with the garment of the happiness in which she was dressed in the days of the life of her man Manasseh,
> καὶ ἔλαβεν σανδάλια εἰς τοὺς πόδας αὐτῆς
> ⁴ and she took sandals on her feet,
> καὶ περιέθετο τοὺς χλιδῶνας καὶ τὰ ψέλια καὶ τοὺς δακτυλίους καὶ τὰ ἐνώτια
> and put around her the bracelets, anklets, finger-rings, and ear-rings,
> καὶ πάντα τὸν κόσμον αὐτῆς
> and all her jewelry,
> καὶ ἐκαλλωπίσατο σφόδρα εἰς ἀπάτησιν ὀφθαλμῶν ἀνδρῶν ὅσοι ἂν ἴδωσιν αὐτήν
> and she beautified (herself) exceedingly for the beguiling of the eyes of the men who would see her.
>
> (Judith 10:3–4)

The detailed description shows Judith's astonishing transformation. The ascetic widow strips off her masculinity and re-genders into the woman that "the eyes of the men" (10:4) expect. This is not the empowering masculine beauty mentioned before (Judith 8:7). I would call it a cosmetically maximised beauty that communicates with the male public, igniting sexual desire and signalling

"God-Wives", "Old Virgins", "Young Widows" 109

availability. Although all the cosmetic embellishment happens on the personal body, it is an act of communication shaping the public body. Soldiers put on armour to prepare for battle; and Judith dons feminine apparel to succeed in her mission. In her preparation prayer, Judith speaks twice of deceitful words (9:10, 13). The nonverbal communication of her outfit communicates enhanced femininity and contributes to the deceitful stratagem.[10] Understanding Judith's beauty-shell as a ruse of war splits her masculinised personal body-concept from her feminine public body. Later, the text confirms this understanding when Judith swears:

ἠπάτησεν αὐτὸν τὸ πρόσωπόν μου εἰς ἀπώλειαν αὐτοῦ καὶ
οὐκ ἐποίησεν ἁμάρτημα μετ' ἐμοῦ εἰς μίασμα καὶ αἰσχύνην
(Judith 13:16)

my face/surface beguiled him to his ruin, and (= but) he committed no sin with me (leading) to defilement and shame.
(Judith 13:16)

Even in the bedroom with the powerful man, Judith maintains her personal body in ascetic masculinity. While Holofernes thought himself master over her attractive feminine body, Judith is the powerful one who takes his life; her strength derives from God, the ultimate power (Judith 13:4):

καὶ προσελθοῦσα τῷ κανόνι τῆς κλίνης ὃς ἦν πρὸς κεφαλῆς
Ολοφέρνου καθεῖλεν τὸν ἀκινάκην αὐτοῦ ἀπ' αὐτοῦ
[6] and going to the bed-post, that was near to Holofernes's head, she took his sword from it,
καὶ ἐγγίσασα τῆς κλίνης ἐδράξατο τῆς κόμης τῆς κεφαλῆς
αὐτοῦ καὶ εἶπεν
[7] and she came close to the bed, seized the hair of his head, and said:
κραταίωσόν με κύριε ὁ θεὸς Ισραηλ ἐν τῇ ἡμέρᾳ ταύτῃ
Empower me Lord, the god of Israel today!
καὶ ἐπάταξεν εἰς τὸν τράχηλον αὐτοῦ δὶς ἐν τῇ ἰσχύι αὐτῆς
καὶ ἀφεῖλεν τὴν κεφαλὴν αὐτοῦ ἀπ' αὐτοῦ
[8] And she struck on his neck twice with (all) her strength and cut his head off from him.

Her taking his hair and using his sword reflects her (masculine) control over him (feminine[11]). He is not the one to grasp her hair (10:3); she grasps his (13:7). He is not the one to dominate her by penetration as he had intended (12:12–16); instead, she uses his own sword to dominate *him*, ultimately killing *him* (13:8). According to the cultural code of masculine domination, this change of roles implies a change of gender. While Judith's public body is masculine, that of Holofernes is feminine. His feminisation, of course, would be even more obvious if she impaled him with the sword. Decapitating him could evoke a symbolic act of castration, though. Anyway, Judith needs his head as a trophy, proving his death, and as a deterrent for display on the city walls (14:1, 11).[12]

Looking back on the role of Judith's singlehood (including her sexual asceticism) it seems to convey at least two messages. First, it communicates a means of self-control that helps Judith to masculinise her public body by keeping her personal body free from sexual domination by a man. Second, it is also a result of social and religious control over her body. God and her people (especially the masculine public) control her sexual purity. While Judith in her heroic deed ignores divine commandments by lying, deceiving, and killing, there are two rules that she respects unconditionally and without compromise: sexual and dietary purity. The latter serves to keep up religio-cultural identity. Avoiding sexual sin also signifies submission and obedience to God; but it conveys yet more. Judith's public statement in 13:16 is also a feminine submission to masculine body control. This ambivalent gender play of a woman masculinising her public body by "virginising" herself in sexual abstinence is necessary under the conditions of masculine domination. As long as sexual intercourse with a man means submitting to his domination, the powerful woman needs to abstain from it – be it marital or extra-marital intercourse. A short look at the writings of the Jewish philosopher Philo confirms this conclusion.

Philo's "Old Virgins" as Wives of Divine Wisdom

In his extensive writings, the Alexandrian author Philo[13] praises asceticism as the ideal way of life. As all passions and pleasures are linked with the earthly, material world, while God is pure spirit, the final goal of human life is to leave behind all material things and to become free for God and spiritual ideas. Given that all Philo's thought is gendered, the human way to perfection is a way of masculinisation: from feminine passion and materialism to masculine reason and divine ideas. This way to the divine means for men that they become more masculine and for women to overcome femininity and achieve masculinity.

In his treaty *De vita contemplativa*, Philo shows up what his concept means in practice by describing an ideal Jewish group that he calls "the Therapeutae: ascetic philosophers, engaged in allegorical exegesis, living in a small community outside the city on the shores of Lake Mareotis" (Taylor & Hay 2020: 6). When Philo describes their meetings, he mentions pure women taking part alongside men:

> (§68) Eating together also are women, who are mostly old virgins, guarding the purity [of this state] not by necessity, as some of the priestesses among the Hellenes do, but rather out of free will. Because of a craving and passion for Sophia/Wisdom, whom they are eager to live with, they have disregarded pleasures connected with a body, yearning not for mortal offspring but for immortal, which the God-loved soul is able to birth alone by herself, when mind-rays of the Father sew in her that which enables her to see the doctrines of Sophia/Wisdom.[14]

With Philo, "virginity" refers to young women before the first menstruation as well as to women after menopause. He automatically links women's bleeding with sexual intercourse, as only fertile women should have sex. Blood and sexual intercourse stand for femininity in the sense of passion, defilement, and earthliness. "Virgins" are free from these defects and, by that, less feminine women. Thus, "virgin" is Philo's keyword for women leaving behind femininity and progressing to masculinity.[15] That is why the female *therapeutae* represent the human soul receiving divine teaching from God. As only virginity grants freedom from bodily desires, it is necessary that the brides of wisdom abstain from men.

Logically, an earthly man fathering human children would not compete with God fathering the knowledge of divine wisdom. As, however, sexuality, body, passions are seen as hindering the openness to God, any person must become free from that as much as possible. The defeminisation of the personal body is the basis for a masculine religious body. Receiving the seed of wisdom, thus excludes any human husband. Women are conceived as being more firmly connected with the femininity of the material world, not least because their bodies are female and associated with blood. Thus, the effort of women to become open to God and to the masculine realms of reason and spirit requires more masculinisation than is the case with men.

For Philo, not rape and sexual domination but *abstaining from sex* constitutes the bodily sacrament of masculine domination. This concept opens a door for women, because it might free them from the domination of a husband and permit them to become part of a *therapeutae* community. However, the price is high, and menstruation and/or sexual activity excluded most women. Even those admitted would not be equal to men in a full sense. Different from Paul, Philo knows no *therapeutae* women in leading functions.

Young "Widows" Promised to Christ

The first Christian document containing the idea of women belonging to Christ as their heavenly husband is the "widows' tale" (Bassler 1984) in 1 Timothy 5:3–16:

> Χήρας τίμα τὰς ὄντως χήρας.
> ³ **Honor (= sponsor) widows, the truly (being) widows!**
> εἰ δέ τις χήρα τέκνα ἢ ἔκγονα ἔχει, μανθανέτωσαν πρῶτον τὸν ἴδιον οἶκον εὐσεβεῖν καὶ ἀμοιβὰς ἀποδιδόναι τοῖς προγόνοις· τοῦτο γάρ ἐστιν ἀπόδεκτον ἐνώπιον τοῦ θεοῦ.
> ⁴ If, however, a widow has children or grandchildren, they should first learn to respect their own house and pay back reward to the parents; for this is adequate in the sight of God.
> ἡ δὲ ὄντως χήρα καὶ μεμονωμένη ἤλπικεν ἐπὶ θεὸν καὶ προσμένει ταῖς δεήσεσιν καὶ ταῖς προσευχαῖς νυκτὸς καὶ ἡμέρας,

⁵ But, **the truly (being) widow and left alone, has hoped on God and remains with supplications and prayers night and day**
ἡ δὲ σπαταλῶσα ζῶσα τέθνηκεν.
⁶ But, the (one) living delightfully (is) a living dead
καὶ ταῦτα παράγγελλε, ἵνα ἀνεπίλημπτοι ὦσιν.
⁷ And this command so that they may be blameless
εἰ δέ τις τῶν ἰδίων καὶ μάλιστα οἰκείων οὐ προνοεῖ, τὴν πίστιν ἤρνηται καὶ ἔστιν ἀπίστου χείρων.
⁸ But if anyone does not provide the own (ones) and especially the members of the household, he/she denies the faith and is worse than an unbeliever
Χήρα καταλεγέσθω μὴ ἔλαττον ἐτῶν ἑξήκοντα γεγονυῖα, ἑνὸς ἀνδρὸς γυνή,
⁹ **A widow should not be listed before being sixty years old**, wife of one man
ἐν ἔργοις καλοῖς μαρτυρουμένη, εἰ ἐτεκνοτρόφησεν, εἰ ἐξενοδόχησεν, εἰ ἁγίων πόδας ἔνιψεν, εἰ θλιβομένοις ἐπήρκεσεν, εἰ παντὶ ἔργῳ ἀγαθῷ ἐπηκολούθησεν.
¹⁰ Testified in good works, if she has brought up children, if she hosted strangers, if she foot-washed saints, if she helped the distressed, if she dedicated herself to every good work.
νεωτέρας δὲ χήρας παραιτοῦ· ὅταν γὰρ καταστρηνιάσωσιν τοῦ Χριστοῦ, γαμεῖν θέλουσιν
¹¹ **but reject younger widows because when they are attracted (emotionally) away from the Christ, they want to marry,**
ἔχουσαι κρίμα ὅτι τὴν πρώτην πίστιν ἠθέτησαν
¹² **having the judgement that they nullified the first commitment/trust.**
ἅμα δὲ καὶ ἀργαὶ μανθάνουσιν περιερχόμεναι τὰς οἰκίας, οὐ μόνον δὲ ἀργαὶ ἀλλὰ καὶ φλύαροι καὶ περίεργοι, λαλοῦσαι τὰ μὴ δέοντα.
¹³ At the same time also (being) useless, they learn going around the houses, not only useless but also gossipy and busybody, saying unnecessary (things).
Βούλομαι οὖν νεωτέρας γαμεῖν, τεκνογονεῖν, οἰκοδεσποτεῖν, μηδεμίαν ἀφορμὴν διδόναι τῷ ἀντικειμένῳ λοιδορίας χάριν·

¹⁴ I want now that the younger marry, give birth, keep house, giving no occasion at all to the adversary for defamation
ἤδη γάρ τινες ἐξετράπησαν ὀπίσω τοῦ σατανᾶ.
¹⁵ for already some have turned off after (= following) the Satan.
εἴ τις πιστὴ ἔχει χήρας, ἐπαρκείτω αὐταῖς καὶ μὴ βαρείσθω ἡ ἐκκλησία, ἵνα ταῖς ὄντως χήραις ἐπαρκέσῃ.
¹⁶ If a believer [female] has widows, she should assist them and the church (may) not be charged so that it can assist the truly (being) widows.

The epistle 1 Timothy belongs together with 2 Timothy and the epistle to Titus to the group of the so-called Pastoral Letters, because their addressees are pastors or congregation leaders. Although these epistles claim Paul as their author, critical research regards them as rather late texts, written long after Paul's death. This is not the place to discuss the pseudo-Pauline origin of the Pastoral Letters, but I would like at least to mention that Pauline theology plays almost no role in these texts. There is also a notable change in the concept of Church, focusing no longer on the congregation as the body of Christ but more on structures similar to the patriarchal household. Annette Merz (2004) aptly calls the Pastoral Letters' use of Paul's name a "fictitious self-interpretation of Paul". As the texts criticise developments that clearly originated from Paul's theology, they have to use his name to confront them. Nobody can correct an apostle like Paul, except Paul himself – hence, the Pauline attribution.

The most obvious correction is in the area of gender and power in the Church. The author's clear intention is to exclude women from power in the Church and to construct a system of offices held by men only. The situation of the Church being addressed seems to be far from the author's ideal. As can be gleaned from the polemics, there is a group of wealthy and well-educated women who hold offices in the Church or at least have authority in teaching and preaching. In her ground-breaking study, Ulrike Wagener (1994) analysed the author's gender strategy as an assimilation of the Church to the model of the patriarchal household. Unfortunately, her study is not well known internationally, although Wagener manages to clear up convincingly the situation in the congregations addressed, which, she argues, betray the patriarchal interests of the authors.

Wagener's reconstruction of an older tradition (marked in bold in my translation above) may be criticised in its details, but at least it delivers a reasonable answer to the question of what the author's problem was. Obviously, the role of an official group of single women (5:3) is at issue. As these women are dedicated to constant prayer, their spiritual status is perhaps comparable to that of Judith. But, their singlehood does not necessarily derive from having lost their husbands. Such biographical details are less important for the "true" widows than their spirituality. The relationship with Christ excludes earthly marriage and the traditional regulation judges the decision to marry as breaking with Christ. To reduce this risk, younger women are excluded from the church's pay roll. According to the traditional material in 1 Timothy 5:3, 5, 9, 11, and 12, "widow" is the name of a congregational spiritual status that seems attractive even for younger women that prefer Christ to any human husband. Already the traditional regulation tries to reduce the number of "widows" by limiting access to elderly women, and pseudo-Paul integrates this regulation into his text. Furthermore, he radicalises the limitation strategy by a huge number of new conditions. In the end, one cannot imagine that *any* woman was left on the Church's pay roll at all. Even a childless, only once married woman over 60, who fulfilled all the moral prerequisites to be listed as a "true" widow, could have found another Christian woman to care for her (5:16). It seems unavoidable but to conclude that the author wants to eliminate church widowhood. His reasons can be gleaned from his polemics[16] against the young widows. If we mirror it, we see spiritual women who use their economic independence (based on Church funding) for pastoral work: they visit people at home, listen and consult, preach, and teach. As the author wants to establish an exclusively male clergy, these women's activities have to be eliminated by othering (cf. Kartzow 2009). As public speech is an aspect of masculine domination, pseudo-Paul condemns women's preaching as especially inappropriate.

> διδάσκειν δὲ γυναικὶ οὐκ ἐπιτρέπω οὐδὲ αὐθεντεῖν ἀνδρός, ἀλλ' εἶναι ἐν ἡσυχίᾳ.
> But I do not permit a woman to teach and not to dominate a man; instead (she has) to be in silence.
>
> (1 Timothy 2:12)

The adequate feminine role is submissive listening but not teaching (cf. 2:11). In order to achieve a patriarchal reconstruction of the Church, pseudo-Paul needs to curtail women's pastoral activity as much as possible. To achieve this, he re-genders the public body of Christian women by assimilating their role to the gender of their personal body. Instead of "usurping" masculinity, they should return to "natural" femininity: that is, to being wife, mother, and housekeeper (5:14). The author not only reconstructs the Church according to the model of the patriarchal household, he also defines the private household as the proper place for women. In 2:15, pseudo-Paul even declares childbirth to be the woman's way to salvation. Such "naturalisation" of feminine subordination is based on a specific interpretation of Genesis 3:1–6 (cf. Küchler): namely, that Eve is guiltier than Adam, as he is but the victim of her seduction (1 Timothy 2:14). Obviously, redemption does not change the status women had since Eve's sin. Whatever might be the effect of salvation according to pseudo-Paul, it cannot touch gender roles. We found such thinking already with Paul himself in 1 Corinthians 11 (see above, Chapter 3), but what was a misogynistic episode there is a misogynistic principle here. The subordination of women is not a consequence of Eve's sin (Genesis 3:16) that is repaired by redemption in Christ. Instead, it is linked with creation itself (1 Timothy 2:13) and is declared to be God's initial will. Thus, the primordial gender hierarchy must be represented "properly" in the structure of the Church. Regarding gender relations, redemption is neither repair of the original sin's consequences, nor new creation. Inferiority and subordination of women is made a primordial structure that is unchangeable. Pseudo-Paul rejects any gender difference between the personal and the religious body; masculine domination is the order of the world and, consequently, that of the Church. The non-Christian patriarchal environment not only delivers the norm for Christian gender politics but is also its judgement used as an argument in Church discussion (cf. 5:14).

Masculine Domination and the Question of Marriage

As patriarchal marriage is an institution to control women, the idea seems plausible that women find more freedom if they avoid marriage. However, a life without a husband may be difficult also, as marriage links women into a society (albeit one dominated by men) in the first place. Therefore, the concept of a heavenly husband, which we have seen with the Egyptian God's wives of Amun, allows some few elite women to achieve high status and influence in society. Although their public body remains feminine, these women achieve power comparable to, and sometimes exceeding, high-ranking men. In past as well as in present times, such models may not be helpful for the vast majority of women. Yet, one has to note that the history of Christianity opened up such models to a broader group of women. Although pseudo-Paul tries to exterminate spiritual widowhood as a way of life, for Christian women later on, being a "bride of Christ" often opened doors to roles of influence and power that were not achievable for married Christian women. Hildegard of Bingen, Teresa of Avila, and many other women could not have played the roles they did if they had been married. Yet, the masculine-dominated Church was usually eager to control such women and their activities (e.g. through individual male confessors) and of course the sexual activity of these women was strictly controlled by Church and society. Living with a divine husband was not an escape from masculine domination. It could not be, because the Church adopted the patriarchal symbolic system of feminine inferiority. Only by their (divine or human) husband, could a woman gain public authority. For those women who agreed to sacrifice their sexual activity, the construction of virginity, widowhood, or of being god's wife was a way to masculinise an aspect of their public body to gain autonomy or power through asceticism. Does this concept contain a positive impulse for women today? This depends very much on cultural context. In western societies offering higher economic independence to women, alongside greater sexual liberty and a notable lack of divine husbands, the idea of being a bride of Christ or any other heavenly husband may not be very popular. In other contexts, however, the model may still hold some liberating potential for women.[17]

Notes

1 The price of such protection was freedom. This was the general structure of monarchy, the most common state-form in antiquity. The rule of the monarch drew its legitimation in large part from the idea that people would be lost without their subordination to the protective, guiding, and nourishing domination of their ruler. For Egypt, see Chapter 1; for later times, see e.g. Veyne (1990).
2 See for example Psalm 68:6; Isaiah 1:17, 23; Jeremiah 22:3; Zechariah 7:10.
3 On the history of this title, see the overview in Shaw and Nicholson (2008: 130–131) and for more detailed information, see Graefe (1981). Ayad (2009a, 2009b, 2016) and most of the contributions in Becker, Blöbaum and Lohwasser (2016) include aspects of gender and power.
4 The suckling scenes (Ayad (2009a: 125, fig. 3.4) assimilate the priestess to the king receiving power in drinking divine milk (see Chapter 1 [Hatshepsut] and Ayad 2009a: 126, fig. 3.5).
5 "Celibacy" of God's wife of Amun just means that there were neither an earthly husband nor legitimate children, but it does not necessarily imply sexual asceticism (cf. Ayad 2009a: 146–152).
6 Only churches (like the Catholic and Orthodox churches), who follow the tradition of the Septuagint, acknowledge the Jewish book of Judith, written in Greek, as a part of their Old Testament.
7 Judith 8:10 informs that all the daily business was under the administration of a special maidservant.
8 Cf. the tent Absalom erects on the palace roof, for raping his father's wives. The tent is visible to the public and his sexual act is a display of his power (2 Samuel 16:22). Cf. Uriah sleeping outside to display his abstinence from sex with his wife Bathsheba (2 Samuel 11:9).

"God-Wives", "Old Virgins", "Young Widows" 119

9 Judith's speeches are even longer than those of Joseph in Genesis 39 (see Chapter 4), and a male audience confirms her wisdom repeatedly.
10 On the transformation of gender roles in the book of Judith, cf. Schmitz (2009) with focus on Judith and Schmitz (2010) with focus on Holofernes.
11 Masculine domination conceives any victim as feminine but in Holofernes's case, the text tells additional attributes of femininity (cf. Schmitz 2010).
12 On the function of displaying a corpse publicly and on the role of Deuteronomy 21:22–23, see Chapter 5.
13 Philo was more or less a contemporary of Jesus and Paul. He stemmed from a prominent family of the important Jewish community in Alexandria (cf. Taylor & Hay 2020: IX–XV).
14 All quotations from Philo's *Vita Contemplativa* follow Taylor and Hay (2020: 75–89).
15 On Philo's construction of femininity, cf. Sly (1990).
16 The big mistake of Tsuji (2001: 102–104) is to read pseudo-Paul's polemics as an adequate description of reality.
17 For an African society like Zimbabwe, see Chitando (2019: 20–21), who talks positively about the Catholic Church having nuns, but also Biri (2021: 81–84), who is more skeptical of the "bride of Christ" concept because of the limitations imposed by the implied asceticism.

7 Zeus-Syndrome, #MeToo, and the Hope for Something New

History is *about* the past but *for* the present. Therefore, I closed each chapter with some tentative perspectives for today based on my understanding of ancient sources. This last chapter cannot sum up all the resonances and reflections that the study of ancient texts brings to the present. Instead, I want to mention a few aspects that seem of importance to me for future developments.

Masculine Domination Is Common but No Ideal

The discussion of multiple sources from different times and religious cultures has informed us amply about the persistence of masculine domination. Many details may be different but the basic juxtaposition of inferior femininity and superior masculinity is a widespread and a trans-cultural phenomenon – including in the Mediterranean world that influenced western cultures so much. Maybe therefore, even today many people think that this gender hierarchy is "natural" or "inevitable". As a follower of Simone de Beauvoir and other feminists, I do not believe it. But even if it were "natural", masculine domination would be as "natural" as the viruses we have to fight against for our survival. The Zeus syndrome has no survival benefit anymore (if it ever did), it kills instead of enriching or securing life.

As I write these lines, millions are tortured by wars and conflicts, initiated and propelled by Zeus-men who sacrifice others' life, well-being, fulfilment, and sexual integrity to the fetish of their own toxic masculinity. The warlords have nothing to contribute for the survival, let alone flourishing, of humanity. They are neither interested nor capable to fight against hunger, injustice, inequality, or climate change.

The costs of Zeus syndrome are high for persons of any gender. Those defined as non-men are marginalized, made helpless, deprived of rights and privileges, suffering violence and death. Those defined by the Zeus syndrome as "real" men are put into the prison of a gender stereotype that leaves only few liberties and destroys the ability of dealing with weakness, non-aggressive emotions, sensibility, and sensuality. Masculine domination puts men, women, and all others into the iron cage of gender definitions. It replaces faith and trust with mistrust and fear; it destroys the hopes of many and through subjugation and sexual violence it produces hatred, anger, and shame instead of love. Therefore, if Christians are willing to focus on the trinity of faith, love, and hope as the traditional icon of human life, they have no option but to fight toxic masculinity.

Women Are Not Only Victims

The survival of eight billion humans requires among other sustainable development goals (SDGs), peace, economic and social justice, protection of minorities, and prevention of further lethal environmental changes. It is obvious that Zeus masculinity has nothing to contribute to any of the seventeen SDGs.[1] The Trumps, Putins, and Bolsonaros of our time do not care for sustainable development for all.

If we talk about toxic masculinity, we have to talk about toxic femininity, too. Masculine domination is not simply some wicked plan of "men" who want to dominate "women". It is a totalitarian cultural system that manipulates persons of any gender. Men, women, and others contribute by their attitudes and actions to the perpetuation of this culture and draw their individual benefits from it along the way. Be it Potiphar's wife, or any First Lady, be it a mother urging her son to kill his sister in the name of family "honour", be it Hatshepsut, or any

Iron Lady adopting masculine power – women are not always innocent victims, many are passively complicit, or willing and strategic collaborators, and some are active perpetrators, blaming victims, defending sexual abusers, permitting their children to be abused, or teaching their daughters to be "real" women, and their boys to be "real" men. Zeus syndrome is not just about a battle of man against woman, it is an all-comprising system influencing all of us, and all will we need a lot of creativity and bold idealism to develop new role models for women, men, and all others. And yet, there is hope: the mere fact that we are discussing masculine domination indicates that this cultural system is no longer subliminal; we can recognize and challenge it and we can imagine life without it. This is an opportunity and an obligation for us all.

Religion Is More Than a Religious Topic

In 2022, humanity seems far off from achieving the sustainable development goals by 2030. The horrible rates of femicide, domestic violence, gender-based abortion of female fetuses, killing of non-heteronormative persons, and similar cruelties inform us that gender justice is for many people a question of life and death. Therefore, it is not just a religious question if powerful religious communities and institutions like the Catholic Church, Orthodox Churches, and many Pentecostals support misogynistic traditions and marginalise non-heteronormative persons. Especially the Catholic Church as the biggest "global player" must commit to a gender politics beyond masculine domination. If the Church means what the Second Vatican Council said, namely that the Church is the instrument of God's love for humankind,[2] then it cannot continue sitting in the lethal shade of patriarchy. Instead, the Church has to become a much more effective fighter for human rights and for the god-given equality of all. However, such a contribution to human development will not be fully trustworthy as long as the bigger half of Catholics are discriminated against within their own Church, through exclusion in terms of fulfilling central religious functions, including those of the priesthood. This is a gender political problem as well as a theological one: as we saw with Paul, the apostolic origins normative for the Church do not support such sexist discrimination.

Sexuality Is Dangerous but Not Evil

Our highly selective journey through the ancient history of the Zeus syndrome informed us about the perils associated with sexuality. Penetration in particular is often deployed as a body-sacrament of masculine domination and as a means to subjugate women (and men). But the generalized demonization of sexuality cultivated by Christianity under Platonist influence is no solution; it is even part of the problem. Rendering sexuality taboo and praising asceticism can sometimes facilitate masculine domination, as we saw with Philo and others. Anti-sexual asceticism *per se* is not a critique of sexual violence if it is not interested in what is suffered by victims. Moreover, desire, lust, and emotion are designated feminine and imply the lessening masculinity. This kind of anti-sexual asceticism – calcified in the celibacy laws for Catholic clergy – is misogynistic by definition, as women are seen as the embodiment of ungodly lust. This association of "evil" femininity and "evil" sexuality did not hinder the true evil of sexual abuse in the Church but fostered it. According to this ideology, the "holy man", as the perfect masculine representation of a perfect masculine and non-sexual God, is authorized to control others' sinful desires through control of his own desires. But such glorification easily becomes toxic when the clerical power is real while control over his own desires is flawed. Because men with uncontrolled power tend to give in to the seductions of the Zeus syndrome, it is harmful to intensify the ideology of priestly asceticism. Sexual abuse always was a sin, even a deadly sin, according to Church doctrine. To repeat this again and again is not enough. We do not need pious mantras but control of power, institutional checks and balances, safeguarding, more transparency, reduction of economic and psychological dependencies, and the eradication of only-men-biotopes in all areas of power – not only in churches and other religious institutions, but also in sports, the arts, business, politics, academia, schools, family, and beyond.

Additionally, we will need to develop a new ethics of sexuality. We need to understand sexuality as both gift and challenge – ambivalent like our rationality and all our other gifts. Not only sexuality, all human talents and abilities, can be used for good and evil. Therefore, it is time to stop tabooing and demonizing sexuality. We have to work on it and configure it as a programme for fostering human life and happiness. If we manage to free sexuality from the grip of the Zeus syndrome, we could finally use it as a language of love, freedom, and responsibility.[3]

What About God?

Christians can contribute to the global humanization of sexuality, if they work on their idea of God, as the ultimate point of orientation for their thinking, feeling, and acting. God is not a super-sized-man legitimating masculine domination. Of course, some biblical texts suggest this, but there are others contradicting them. We have to focus more on the contradictions within the Bible and cherish them as signals of hope. When we see cracks and rifts in the surface of the Zeus syndrome and see something different that is not yet reality but already shimmering through, then we see a chance. God can be detected as the ultimate counterbalance to the status quo, the last question mark. If we understand that God is less about certainty than challenge, we will embrace all the cracks in the gender stereotypes of masculine domination that so many biblical texts offer.

"I am God and not man" (Hosea 11:9) – God is more than the legitimation of machismo and rape culture. Not only a suffering, ugly messiah transcends traditional clichés of masculinity, the Father also is rather queer, transcending gender stereotypes in divine sovereignty. God is not Zeus; Jesus is not Herakles; Mary is not Leda (cf. Koet & Peerbolte 2022); and the Holy Spirit is neither a swan nor an eagle. As our religious language often tends to forget this, we should perhaps use and emphasize "other" pronouns and attributes for God. If God is our mother, then *he* is a strong helper and leader. If God is our father, then *she* sent *her* son to speak of *her* love. Such "wrong" linguistic gender mixing is not yet a solution. However, it is keeping questions unanswered and open questions are our hope and our freedom.

Notes

1. On the SDGs, see https://sdgs.un.org/goals (accessed 13/04/2022).
2. Cf. "Dogmatic Constitution on the Church" *Lumen Gentium 1* (https://www.vatican.va/archive/hist_councils/ii_vatican_council/documents/vat-ii_const_19641121_lumen-gentium_en.html [accessed 13/04/2022]).
3. Gunda (2010: 141) quotes Archbishop Desmond Tutu (1931-2021) saying, "sexuality is a divine gift, which when used properly, helps us to become more fully human and akin really to God".

Bibliography

Ackerman, Susan. 1998. *Warrior, Dancer, Seductress, Queen: Women in Judges and Biblical Israel*. New York: Doubleday.
Angenendt, Arnold. 1997. *Geschichte der Religiosität im Mittelalter*. Darmstadt: Wiss. Buchges.
Assmann, Jan. 1982. Die Zeugung des Sohnes. In: J. Assmann, W. Burkert & F. Stolz (Eds.). *Funktionen und Leistungen des Mythos*. Freiburg: Universitätsverlag, pp. 13–61.
─── 1984. *Ägypten: Theologie und Frömmigkeit einer frühen Hochkultur*. Stuttgart: Kohlhammer.
─── 1990. *Ma'at. Gerechtigkeit und Unsterblichkeit im alten Ägypten*. Munich: Beck.
─── 2011. 'Maʿat'. In: *Religion Past and Present*. http://dx.doi.org/10.1163/1877-5888_rpp_SIM_13311 (accessed 25/10/2021).
Ayad, Mariam F. 2009a. *God's Wife, God's Servant: The God's Wife of Amun (c. 740–525 BC)*. London: Routledge.
─── 2009b. The Transition from Libyan to Nubian Rule: The Role of the God's Wife of Amun. In: G.P.F. Broekman, R.J. Demarée & O.E. Kaper (Eds.). *The Libyan Period in Egypt*. Leuven: Peeters, pp. 29–49.
─── 2016. Gender, Ritual, and Manipulation of Power. The God's Wife of Amun (Dynasty 23–26). In: M. Becker, A.I. Blöbaum & A. Lohwasser (Eds.). *"Prayer and Power". Proceedings of the Conference on the God's Wives of Amun in Egypt during the First Millennium BC*. Münster: Ugarit, pp. 89–106.
Bagnall, Roger S. (Ed.). 2021. *Roman Egypt: A History*. Cambridge: CUP.
Bassler, Jouette M. 1984. The Widows' Tale: A Fresh Look at 1 Tim 5:3–16. In: *Journal of Biblical Literature* 103, pp. 23–41.
Beauvoir, Simone de. 2011 [1949]. *The Second Sex*. London: Vintage.

Bechmann, Ulrike. 2000. Duft im Alten Testament. In: J. Kügler et al. (Eds.). *Die Macht der Nase*. Stuttgart: kbw, pp. 49–98.

Beck, Stefanie. 2020. *Witwen und Bibel in Tansania: eine leserinnenorientierte Lektüre von 1 Tim* 5:3-16 Bamberg: UBP.

Becker, Meike, Blöbaum, Anke Ilona & Lohwasser, Angelika (Eds.). 2016. *"Prayer and Power". Proceedings of the Conference on the God's Wives of Amun in Egypt during the First Millennium BC*. Münster: Ugarit.

Biri, Kudzai. 2021. *"The Wounded Beast?" – Single Women, Tradition, and the Bible in Zimbabwe*. Bamberg: UBP.

Böhler, Dieter. 2021. *Psalmen 1-50*. Freiburg: Herder.

Borg, Barbara. 1998. *"Der zierlichste Anblick der Welt …". Ägyptische Porträtmumien*. Mainz: Zabern.

Bormann, Lukas. 2008. Visuelle Kommunikation des Evangeliums. In: J. Kügler & L. Bormann (Eds.). *Töchter (Gottes)*. Berlin: Lit, pp. 101–112.

Bourdieu, Pierre. 2001. *Masculine Domination*. Cambridge: Polity Press.

Bowman, Alan K. 1986. *Egypt after the Pharaohs*. London: British Museum.

Brasch, Thomas. 1982. *Rede zur Verleihung des Bayerischen Filmpreises*. https://www.zeit.de/1982/04/rede-zur-verleihung-des-bayerischen-filmpreises (accessed 05/04/2022).

Breasted, James Henry. 1906. *Ancient Records of Egypt II*. Chicago: UCP.

Brunner, Hellmut. 1986. *Die Geburt des Gottkönigs. Studien zur Überlieferung eines altägyptischen Mythos*. 2nd edition. Wiesbaden: Harrassowitz.

Brunner-Traut, Emma. 1977. 'Geierhaube'. In: *Lexikon der Ägyptologie II*. Wiesbaden: Harrassowitz, p. 515.

Bryan, Betsy M. 2000. The 18th Dynasty before the Amarna Period (c.1550–1352 BC). In: I. Shaw (Ed.). *The Oxford History of Ancient Egypt*. Oxford: OUP, pp. 218–271.

Budge, E. A. Wallis. 1994 [1912]. *Legends of the Egyptian Gods*. New York: Dover.

Bynum, Caroline Walker. 1992. *Fragmentation and Redemption*. New York: Zone.

Carden, Michael. 2006. 'Genesis/Bereshit'. In: D. Guest et al. (Eds.). *The Queer Bible Commentary*. London: SCM, pp. 21–60.

Casagrande-Kim, Roberta (Ed.). 2014. *When the Greeks ruled Egypt. From Alexander the Great to Cleopatra*. New York: ISAW.

Chapman, Cynthia R. 2004. *The Gendered Language of Warfare in the Israelite-Assyrian Encounter*. Winona Lake: Eisenbrauns.

Chitando, Ezra. 2019. Introduction: The Bible, the Church, and Gender Troubles in Africa. In: J. Kügler, R. Gabaitse & J. Stiebert (Eds.). *The Bible and Gender Troubles in Africa*. Bamberg: UBP, pp. 13–24.

Chitando, Ezra & Chirongoma, Sophia (Eds). 2013. *Justice Not Silence: Churches Facing Sexual and Gender-based Violence*. Stellenbosch: Sun Press.

Clines, David J. A. 1995. *Interested Parties: The Ideology of Writers and Readers of the Hebrew Bible*. Sheffield: SAP.

Cohen, Edward E. 2014. Sexual Abuse and Sexual Rights. In: T.K. Hubbard (Ed.). *A Companion to Greek and Roman Sexualities*. Chichester: Wiley-Blackwell, pp. 188–202.

Cook, John Granger. 2014. *Crucifixion in the Mediterranean World*. Tübingen: Mohr-Siebeck.

Coşkun, Altay (Ed.). 2016. *Seleukid Royal Women*. Stuttgart: Steiner.

Dassmann, Ernst. 1997. 'Non decet neque necessarium est …'. In: *Projekttag Frauenordination*. Bonn: Borengässer, pp. 52–65.

Deminion, Mary. 2020. Manly and Monstrous Women: (De-)Constructing Gender in Roman Oratory. In: A. Surtees & J. Dyer (Eds.). *Exploring Gender Diversity in the Ancient World*. Edinburgh: EUP, pp. 197–208.

Dietrich, Jan. 2019. Wisdom in the Cultures of the Ancient World: A General Introduction and Comparison. In: T.M. Oshima, with S. Kohlhaas (Eds.). *Teaching Morality in Antiquity*. Tübingen: Mohr-Siebeck, pp. 3–18.

Edwards, Catherine (Ed.). 2000. *Suetonius: Lives of Caesars*. Oxford: OUP.

Ebach, Jürgen. 2007. *Genesis 37-50*. Freiburg: Herder.

Exum, J. Cheryl. 2005. *Song of Songs*. Louisville: Westminster John Knox.

Figueroa, Rocio & Tombs, David. 2020. *Seeing His Innocence, I See My Innocence: Responses from Abused Nuns to Jesus as a Victim of Sexual Abuse*. www.academia.edu/42147523 (accessed 11/04/2022).

Finkelstein, Israel & Silberman, Neil A. 2007. David and Solomon. In: *Search of the Bible's Sacred Kings and the Roots of the Western Tradition*. New York: Free Press.

Foucault, Michel. 1978. *The History of Sexuality*, 3 vols. New York: Pantheon Books.

Francis, Pope. 2013. *Apostolic Exhortation Evangelii Gaudium* http://w2.vatican.va/content/francesco/en/apost_exhortations/documents/papa-francesco_esortazione-ap_20131124_evangelii-gaudium.html (accessed 11/04/2022).

Gerleigner, Georg Simon. 2016. Tracing Letters on the Eurymedon Vase: On the Importance of Placement of Vase-Inscriptions. In:

D. Yatromanolakis (Ed.). *Epigraphy of Art. Ancient Greek Vase-Inscriptions and Vase-Paintings*. Oxford: Archaeopress, pp. 165–184.

—— 2017. Rolle und Bedeutung der Frau: "In den Gemeinden sollen die Frauen schweigen" (1 Kor 14,34). In: *Zur Debatte*. Sonderheft zur Ausgabe 1/2017, pp. 12 f.

Gielen, Marlis & Kügler, Joachim (Eds.). 2014. *Papst Franziskus und die Zukunft der Kirche*. Berlin: Lit.

Glazebrook, Allison & Olson, Kelly. 2014. Greek and Roman marriage. In: T.K. Hubbard (Ed.). *A Companion to Greek and Roman Sexualities*. Chichester: Wiley-Blackwell, pp. 73–86.

Goitein, S.D. 1993 [1957]. The Song of Songs: A Female Composition. In: A. Brenner (Ed.). *A Feminist Companion to the Song of Songs*. Sheffield: SAP, pp. 58–66.

Goldingay, John & Payne, David. 2006. *A Critical and Exegetical Commentary on Isaiah 40-55. II. Commentary on Isaiah 44:24-55:13*. London: T&T Clark.

Greenough, Chris. 2021. *The Bible and Sexual Violence Against Men*. London: Routledge.

Graefe, Erhart. 1981. *Untersuchungen zur Verwaltung und Geschichte der Institution der Gottesgemahlin des Amun vom Beginn des Neuen Reiches bis zur Spätzeit*, 2 vols. Wiesbaden: Harrassowtz.

Grimm, Alfred & Schoske, Sylvia. 1999. *Hatschepsut: KönigIn Ägyptens*. Munich: SMÄK.

Gunda, Masiiwa Ragies. 2010. *The Bible and Homosexuality in Zimbabwe*. Bamberg: UBP.

Hagedorn, Anselm. 2018 [2006]. 'Hoheslied'. *Wibilex*, permalink: https://www.bibelwissenschaft.de/stichwort/21454/ (accessed 11/04/2022).

Hallett, Judith P. 1984. *Fathers and Daughters in Roman Society*. Princeton: PUP.

Hannig, Rainer. 1997. *Die Sprache der Pharaonen. Großes Handwörterbuch Ägyptisch-Deutsch (2800-950 v. Chr.)*. 2nd edition. Mainz: Zabern.

Heath, Elaine A. 2011. *We Were the Least of These: Reading the Bible with Survivors of Sexual Abuse*. Grand Rapids: Brazos.

Hengel, Martin. 1993. "Setze dich zu meiner Rechten!". Die Inthronisation Christi zur Rechten Gottes und Psalm 110,1. In: M. Philonenko (Ed.). *Le Trône de Dieu*. Tübingen: Mohr Siebeck.

Hieke, Thomas. 2015. Kennt und verurteilt das Alte Testament Homosexualität? In: S. Goertz (Ed.). *"Wer bin ich, ihn zu verurteilen?" – Homosexualität und katholische Kirche*. Freiburg: Herder, pp. 19–52.

Hornung, Erik & Staehelin, Elisabeth. 2006. *Neue Studien zum Sedfest*. Basel: Schwabe.

https://www.brooklynmuseum.org/exhibitions/womans_afterlife_ ancient_egypt (accessed 16/10/2021). <*A Woman's Afterlife: Gender Transformation in Ancient Egypt*, exhibition organized by Edward Bleiberg, Curator of Egyptian Art, Brooklyn Museum, New York>.

Hubbard, Thomas K. 2014. Peer Homosexuality. In: T.K. Hubbard (Ed.). *A Companion to Greek and Roman Sexualities*. Chichester: Wiley-Blackwell, pp. 132–153.

James, Sharon L. & Dillon, Sheila. 2012. *A Companion to Women in the Ancient World*. Chichester: Wiley-Blackwell.

Junge, Friedrich. 1995. Die Erzählung vom Streit der Götter Horus und Seth um die Herrschaft. In: *Texte aus der Umwelt des Alten Testaments III*. Gütersloh: Gütersloher Verlagshaus, pp. 930–950.

Jussen, Bernhard 2009. The King's Two Bodies Today. In: *Representations* 106/1, pp. 102–117.

Kantorowicz, Ernst H. 1957. *The King's Two Bodies*. Princeton: PUP.

Kartzow, Marianne Bjelland. 2009. *Gossip and Gender. Othering of Speech in the Pastoral Epistles*. Berlin: De Gruyter.

Koet, Bart J. & Lietaert Peerbolte, Bert Jan. 2022. The Annunciation Narrative (Luke 1:27-38) Read in Times of #MeToo. In: *Biblische Notizen* 192, pp. 91–103.

Küchler, Max. 1986. *Schweigen, Schmuck und Schleier*. Göttingen: V&R.

Kügler, Joachim. 1997. *Pharao und Christus?* Bodenheim: Philo.

―――― 2011. Wenn der Messias so stirbt. In: S. Knaeble, S. Wagner & V. Wittmann (Eds.). *Gott und Tod. Tod und Sterben in der höfischen Kultur des Mittelalters*. Berlin: Lit, pp. 331–346.

―――― 2013. In the Cobra's Back. Why It Would Perhaps Be Better to Read the Bible as Literature. In: J. Kügler & M.R. Gunda (Eds.). *From Text to Practice*. 2nd edition. Bamberg: UBP, pp. 184–217.

―――― 2017. *Exegese zwischen Religionsgeschichte und Pastoral*. Stuttgart: kbw.

―――― 2019. Paul and the Prophetic Christian Women of Corinth. In: J. Kügler, R. Gabaitse & J. Stiebert (Eds.). *The Bible and Gender Troubles in Africa*. Bamberg: UBP, pp. 239–257.

―――― 2020. Jesus als Opfer sexuellen Missbrauchs? https://www.academia.edu/43596019 (accessed 11/04/2022).

―――― 2021. *Sexualität – Macht – Religion. Zeitreisen ins Bermuda-Dreieck menschlicher Existenz*. Würzburg: Echter.

Kyne, Will (Ed.). 2021. *The Oxford Handbook of Wisdom and the Bible*. New York: OUP.

Lembke, Katja. 1994. *Das Iseum Campense in Rom. Studie über den Isiskult unter Domitian*. Heidelberg: Archäologie & Geschichte.

Leutzsch, Martin. 2004. Konstruktionen von Männlichkeit im Urchristentum. In: F. Crüsemann et al. (Eds.). *Dem Tod nicht glauben. Sozialgeschichte der Bibel.* Gütersloh: Gütersloher Verlagshaus, pp. 600–618.

Lichtheim, Miriam. 1975. 1976. *Ancient Egyptian Literature. I, II.* Berkeley: UCP.

Lings, K. Renato. 2009. The "Lyings" of a Woman: Male-Male Incest in Leviticus 18.22? In: *Theology & Sexuality* 15, pp. 231–250.

Lüke, Ulrich. 2018. Jesu Männlichkeit oder Jesu Menschlichkeit? In: *Theologische Quartalschrift* 198, pp. 183–199.

MacDonald, Nathan. 2019. The Priestly Vestments. In: C. Berner et al. (Eds.). *Clothing and Nudity in the Hebrew Bible.* New York: T&T Clark, pp. 435–448.

McKay, Heather. 2017. Clothing, Adornment and Accouterments as Cultural and Literary Signifiers in the 'Historical' Books. In: A. Brenner-Idan & A.C.C. Lee (Eds.). *Samuel, Kings and Chronicles, I: Texts@Contexts.* London: Bloomsbury T&T Clark, pp. 238–252.

Manyonganise, Molly. 2016. Zimbabweans and the Prophetic Frenzy: Fertile Ground for Women's Sexual Abuse? In: J. Hunter & J. Kügler (Eds.). *The Bible and Violence in Africa.* Bamberg: UBP, pp. 269–283.

Martinet, Hans (Hg.). 2006. *C. Suetonius Tranquillus, Die Kaiserviten/ De Vita Caesarum – Berühmte Männer/De Viris Illustribus. Lateindeutsch.* 3rd edition. Düsseldorf: Artemis & Winkler.

Matić, Uroš. 2021. *Violence and Gender in Ancient Egypt.* London: Routledge.

Meier, John P. 2001. A Marginal Jew: Rethinking the Historical Jesus. Vol. III. *Companions and Competitors.* New York: Doubleday.

Melaerts, Henri (Ed.). 2002. *Le rôle et le statut de la femme en Egypte hellénistique, romaine et byzantine.* Leuven: Peeters.

Merklein, Helmut. 1983. "Es ist gut für den Menschen, eine Frau nicht anzufassen". Paulus und die Sexualität nach 1 Kor 7. In: G. Dautzenberg, H. Merklein & K. Müller (Eds.). *Die Frau im Urchristentum.* Freiburg: Herder, pp. 225–253.

——— 1997. Zur Stichhaltigkeit der exegetischen Begründungsverfahren in "Inter insigniores" und "Ordinatio sacerdotalis". In: *Projekttag Frauenordination.* Bonn: Borengässer, pp. 39–51.

Merz, Annette. 2004. *Die fiktive Selbstauslegung des Paulus.* Göttingen: V&R.

Naville, Edouard. 1896. 1898. 1901. *The Temple of Deir el Bahari, Part II, III, IV.* London: Egypt Exploration Fund.

Neils, Jenifer. 2011. *Women in the Ancient World.* London: British Museum Press.

Nissinen, Martti. 1998. *Homoeroticism in the Biblical World.* Minneapolis: Fortress Press.
Ordination of Women 3. Christianity. https://en.wikipedia.org/wiki/Ordination_of_women#Christianity (accessed 11/04/2022).
Pedrucci, Giulia (Ed.). 2019. *Breastfeeding(s) and Religions.* Rome: Scienze e Lettere.
Pilhava, Kaisa-Maria. 2017. *Forgotten Women Leaders.* Helsinki: Finnish Exegetical Society.
Punt, Jeremy. 2016. The Bible and Others: Root of Violence in Africa? In: J. Hunter & J. Kügler (Eds.). *The Bible and Violence in Africa.* Bamberg: UBP, pp. 35–57.
Quirke, Stephen. 1994. Translating Ma'at. In: *The Journal of Egyptian Archaeology* 80, pp. 219–231.
Reaves, Jayme R. & Tombs, David. 2019. #MeToo Jesus: Naming Jesus as a Victim of Sexual Abuse. In: *International Journal of Public Theology* 13, pp. 387–412.
Reinsberg, Carola. 1989. *Ehe, Hetärentum und Knabenliebe im antiken Griechenland.* München: Beck.
Robins, Gay. 1996. Dress, Undress, and the Representation of Fertility and Potency in New Kingdom Egyptian Art. In: N.B. Kampen (Ed.). *Sexuality in Ancient Art: Near East, Egypt, Greece, and Italy.* Cambridge: CUP, pp. 27–40.
Roehrig, Catharine H. with Dreyfus, Renée & Keller, Cathleen A. (Eds.). 2005. *Hatshepsut: from Queen to Pharaoh.* New Haven: YUP.
Römer, Thomas. 2019. Genesis 39 and the Composition of the Joseph Narrative. In: *Hebrew Bible and Ancient Israel* 8, pp. 44–60.
Rößler-Köhler, Ursula. 1991. *Individuelle Haltungen zum ägyptischen Königtum der Spätzeit.* Wiesbaden: Harrassowitz.
Ryan, Scott C. 2019. *Divine Conflict and the Divine Warrior: Listening to Romans and Other Jewish Voices.* Tübingen: Mohr Siebeck.
Schäfer, Peter. 2010. *Geschichte der Juden in der Antike.* 2nd edition. Tübingen: Mohr Siebeck.
Scherer, Hildegard. 2016. Die Mühe der Frauen. In: *Biblische Zeitschrift* 60, pp. 264–276.
Schipper, Bernd U. 2019. The Egyptian Background of the Joseph Story. In: *Hebrew Bible and Ancient Israel* 8, pp. 6–23.
—————— 2021. *A Concise History of Ancient Israel.* University Park: PSUP.
Schmitz, Barbara. 2009. Casting Judith. The Construction of Role Patterns in the Book of Judith. In: H. Lichtenberger (Ed.). *Biblical Figures in Deuterocanonical and Cognate Literature.* Berlin: De Gruyter, pp. 77–94.

――― 2010. Holofernes' Canopy in the Septuagint. In: K.R. Brine, E. Ciletti & H. Lähnemann (Eds.). *The Sword of Judith*. Cambridge: Open Book

Schmitz, Barbara & Engel, Helmut. 2014. *Judit*. Freiburg: Herder.

Schneider, Thomas. 1994. *Lexikon der Pharaonen*. Zürich: Artemis.

Schnelle, Udo. 2003. *Paulus. Leben und Denken*. Berlin: de Gruyter.

Schreiber, Stefan. 2000. Arbeit mit der Gemeinde (Röm 16:6,12). Zur versunkenen Möglichkeit der Gemeindeleitung durch Frauen. In: *New Testament Studies* 46, pp. 204–226.

Schroer, Silvia. 1992. *Die Samuelbücher*. Stuttgart: kbw.

――― 2005. *Die Ikonographie Palästinas/Israels und der Alte Orient 1*. Fribourg: Academic Press.

Seidl, Theodor. 2018 [2009]. "Heiligkeitsgesetz". *WiBiLex*, permalink: http://www.bibelwissenschaft.de/de/stichwort/20857/ (accessed 11/04/2022).

Shaw, Ian & Nicholson, Paul. 2008. *The British Museum Dictionary of Ancient Egypt, revised and expanded edition*. London: British Museum Press.

Shirun-Grumach, Irene. 1993. *Offenbarung, Orakel und Königsnovelle*. Wiesbaden: Harrassowitz.

Sly, Dorothy I. 1990. *Philo's Perception of Women*. Atlanta: Scholars Press.

Smith, Mark. 2017. *Following Osiris: Perspectives on the Osirian Afterlife from Four Millenia*. Oxford: OUP.

Smoak, Jeremy D. 2021. Building Solomon's Temple: Crafting a Monumental Inventory in I Kgs 7:13–47. In: *Hebrew Bible and Ancient Israel* 10, pp. 283–300.

Stavrianopoulou, Eftychia. 2006. *"Gruppenbild mit Dame": Untersuchungen zur rechtlichen und sozialen Stellung der Frau auf den Kykladen im Hellenismus und in der römischen Kaiserzeit*. Stuttgart: Steiner.

Sternberg-el-Hotabi, Heike. 1988. Balsamierungsritual pBoulaq3. In: *Texte aus der Umwelt des Alten Testaments II.3*. Gütersloh: Gütersloher Verlagshaus, pp. 405–431.

Stiebert, Johanna. 2016. *First-degree Incest and the Hebrew Bible: Sex in the Family*. London: Bloomsbury T&T Clark.

――― 2019. The Wife of Potiphar. Sexual Harassment and False Rape Allegation. In: J. Kügler, R. Gabaitse & J. Stiebert (Eds.). *The Bible and Gender Troubles in Africa*. Bamberg: UBP, pp. 73–114.

――― 2020. *Rape Myths, the Bible and #MeToo*. London: Routledge.

Taylor, Joan E. & Hay, David M. (Eds.). 2020. *Philo of Alexandria: On the Contemplative Life*. Leiden: Brill.

Thiede, Barbara. 2022. *Rape Culture in the House of David: A Company of Men*. London: Routledge.
Thraede, Klaus. 1972. 'Frau'. In: *Reallexikon für Antike und Christentum VIII*. Stuttgart: Hiersemann, pp. 197–269.
Tielesch, Simon. 2013. Der schöne Mann im Alten Testament. Untersuchungen zu Hld 5,10-16. In: *Biblische Notizen* 157, pp. 33–67.
Tobin, Thomas H. 1992. 'Logos'. In: *Anchor Bible Dictionary IV*. New York: Doubleday.
Tombs, David. 1999. Crucifixion, State Terror, and Sexual Abuse. In: *Union Seminary Quarterly Review* 53, pp. 89–109.
——— 2017. Review of Granger Cook, Crucifixion in the Mediterranean World. In: *The Bible & Critical Theory* 13, pp. 103–107.
Trainor, Michael. 2014. *The Body of Jesus and Sexual Abuse*. Eugene: Wipf & Stock Publishers.
Trebilco, Paul R. 1991. *Jewish Communities in Asia Minor*. Cambridge: CUP.
Tsuji, Manabu. 2001. Zwischen Ideal und Realität. Zu den Witwen in 1 Tim 5,3-13. *New Testament Studies* 47, pp. 92–104.
Tyldesley, Joyce. 1996. *Hatchepsut: The Female Pharaoh*. London: Viking.
Vengeyi, Elizabeth. 2016. The Bible, Violence, Women, and African Initiated Churches in Zimbabwe. In: J. Hunter & J. Kügler (Eds.). *The Bible and Violence in Africa*. Bamberg: UBP, pp. 257–268.
Veyne, Paul. 1990. *Bread and Circuses: Historical Sociology and Political Pluralism*. London: Lane.
Vössing, Konrad. 2004. *Mensa Regia: Das Bankett beim hellenistischen König und beim römischen Kaiser*. München/Leipzig: Saur.
Wagener, Ulrike. 1994. *Die Ordnung des "Hauses Gottes". Der Ort von Frauen in der Ekklesiologie und Ethik der Pastoralbriefe*. Tübingen: Mohr-Siebeck.
Wagner, Thomas. 2020 [2012]. 'Israel (AT)'. *WiBiLex*, permalink: https://www.bibelwissenschaft.de/stichwort/21934/ (accessed 11/04/2022).
Wilson, Stephen M. 2015. *Making Men: The Male Coming-of-Age Theme in the Hebrew Bible*. New York: OUP.
Zenger, Erich & Hossfeld, Frank-Lothar. 1993. Die Psalmen I. *Psalm 1-50*. Würzburg: Echter.
Zimunya, Clive Tendai & Gwara, Joyline. 2019. "Do not touch my anointed!" (Ps 105) – An Analysis of Sexual Violations in Zimbabwean Religious Movements. In: J. Kügler, R. Gabaitse, & J. Stiebert (Eds.). *The Bible and Gender Troubles in Africa*. Bamberg: UBP, pp. 115–128.

Index

Page numbers followed by "n" refer to notes.

Aaron 101n12
abomination 70, 73
Absalom 87, 89; masculinity 89; sex with his father's secondary wives 89
Acts of the Apostles: 8:27–35 94; 13:33 101n20
agape (selfless love) 7
Agrippa I 36
Ahab 68
Ahmose 21
Alexander 60
all others (persons of all genders and sexes) 11n1, 75
alternative sexual norm 75
Amenirdi 105
Amun 18, 20–22, 28, 104–105, 117, 118n5
Amun-Re 14
Amun-Zeus 104
Antiochia 35
Antiochian-Pauline influence 39
anti-sexual asceticism 123
Antony, Marc 63
asceticism 123
Assmann, Jan 24
Assyrian empire 68
Augustus 63, 67n25

Augustus of Prima Porta 101n17
Ayad, Mariam F. 118n3

baptised Christians 35
baptism 34–39, 42
Bathsheba 89, 118n8
beauty of anointed king 89–91; hero's power-beauty 86–89; masculine beauty 84–86; ugly redeemer 91–94
Beauvoir, Simone de 7, 120
Becker, Meike 118n3
biblical marital ideals 82n15
Biri, Kudzai 119n17
Birth Cycle 21–22, 24
Bithynia 66n21
blasphemy 67n28
Blöbaum, Anke Ilona 118n3
bodily masculinisation 18
body of Christ 6
book of Leviticus. 9
Bourdieu, Pierre 7, 12n5
bride of Christ 117
Budge, E. A. Wallis 28n3
bull palette *52*, 53

Caesar, Gaius Julius 61–62; sexual activity 63
Caligula 63

Index

Canaan 74
Carden, Michael 82n19
Catholic Church 1
Catholicism 1; *see also* Christian/Christianity
Chapman, Cynthia 100n10
child abuse 1
child-abuse scandals in churches 2
children of God 36
Chitando, Ezra 119n17
Christian/Christianity 6; congregation 38; congregation in Corinth 42; demonization of sexuality 123; widowhood 9
churches: of Antiochia 46n11; child-abuse scandals in 2; funding 115; male leaders 98; masculinity 40–41, 98, 117; pay roll 115; public Church body 5; roles and functions 43; Roman Catholic Church 42–43, 47n24; structures 1
Church masculinity 40; *see also* masculine domination
Cicero 92
Clines, David J. A. 85
clothing of the king 36
conservative-to-fundamentalist 64
Cook, John Granger 101n14
1 Corinthians 47n23; 1:17 92; 1:23 92; 4:33b–36 47n21; 7:1 47n23; 11 41, 116; 11:2–16 40, 46n18, 47n20; 11:4–5 41, 46n18; 11:14 41; 11:15 41; 12 41; 12:27 38; 14:33b–36 46n18; 15:5–8 94
Coşkun, Altay 46n16
crucifixion 9, 91–94, 98, 101n14; decay 92; display 92; duration 92; forced nakedness 92; Jesus 93–94; torture 92

Daniel 86; 1:4 86
Dassmann, Ernst 48n26
daughters of God 37, 81n11
David 87; Michal's love for 89; rape culture 89; sexual conduct 89
defeminisation of personal body 111
Deir el-Bahari 20–23
de-masculinisation 93
Deutero-Isaiah 95
Deuteronomy: 5:21 79; 21:22–23 93, 119n12; 21:23 93
deutero-Pauline intensification 42
divine masculinity 95; *see also* masculinity/masculinisation
divine milk 24
divine paternity 20
Djeser Djeseru 19–20, 22
Domitianus, Titus Flavius 16

Ebach, Jürgen 82n15, 83n23
Egypt 74
Egyptian gods 49–55
Egyptian kingship, gender of 13–14
Egyptian Merneptah-Stele 80n1
Egyptian royal iconography 19
Ephesians: 5:22–33 42
eros (desire/affection) 7
erotic love 84
eunuch 81n12
Eurymedon-vase 56, *56*
Eve's sin 116
Exodus: 4:16 101; 7:1 101

femininity/feminisation 49, 59, 63, 75, 111; in Greek city states 37; in Hellenistic-Roman time 37; inferiority 117; of men 8; of public body 54, 97; public patronage 37; religion-based singlehood 10
Flavius, Josephus 92
Foucault, Michel 7

Galatians: 3 38, 41–42; 3:26–28 34; 3:27–28 35
Galba 60

Index

Gallia 61
Gallic tribes 62
Ganymede 11n2, 64
gay 70
Geburtszyklus 18
gender: code of ancient culture 95; hierarchy 7, 82n20; justice 44; neutral Church practices 38; neutrality 38; politics 122; significance of clothing 36; undifferentiated salvation 44
gender-ambiguous persons 98
Genesis: 1:3 82n20; 1:6 82n20; 1:9 82n20; 1:11 82n20; 1:14 82n20; 1:20 82n20; 1:24 82n20; 1:26 82n20; 3:1–6 116; 19 70; 37 82n19; 37–50 79; 39 76, 79–80, 81n12, 83n24–83n25, 119n9; 39:6 76; 39:7 76–77, 82n20; 39:8–9 78; 39:10 76–77, 82n20; 39:12 77–78; 41:40 82n21
Gerleigner, Georg Simon 57, 66n13
Gibeah 72
Gielen, Marlis 46n18
Glazebrook, Allison 82n15
goddesses 22
God/gods 91, 124–125; active presence 91; identity of 74; people of 73–74; suffering servant of 94; supreme power 6; God's power 89–91
god-king 91
Goliath 88
Graefe, Erhart 118n3
Greek masculinity 57
Greek Zeus-Syndrome 55–60
Greenough, Chris 102n23
Gunda, Masiiwa Ragies 80n3, 125n3

Harpocrates 45n3
Hathor (of) NN 20, 23–25, 33; mother of Horus 24

Hatshepsut 8, 13–14; daughter of god 21–23; daughter of goddess 23–25; daughter of king 19–21; declared king 16–19; dynastic context of reign 14–16; eternity 25–26; female identity 25; gender adaption 18; genders 24–25; king of Egypt 18; kingship to feminine 17; kingship with Amun king of gods 21; masculine iconography 18, 105; masculinity of the king 17; mortuary temple at Deir el-Bahari 20; mytho-political strategy 20; parent-daughter relations 20; personal body 18–19; pornographic graffito 26; public body 18; re-gendering 18; royal iconography 17, 20; sex and gender of 18; traditional masculinity of the king 17; vice-regent for Thutmose III 20; vice-regent of child-king Thutmose III 15–16
Heath, Elaine A. 99, 102n23
Hebrew Bible 7
Hebrew slave 77
Hellenistic kings 44n2
Hellenistic-Roman Egypt 32–33, 37
Hera 58
Herakles 58
Herodotus 104
Hieke, Thomas 80n3
Hildegard of Bingen 117
hippie-movement 2
ḥmt nswt wrt 14
Holiness Code 70, 73, 83n24
Holofernes 110
Holy Spirit 124
homoerotic attraction 86
homosexuality 9, 70
honor 112

Horus 12n4, 13, 49; incarnation of 13; myth 49; non-royal individuals on role 33
Horus-Osiris-concept 25
Hosea: 11:9 124
human-made system 54
husband-wife relationship 105

inferior femininity 120
intra-dynastic marriages 14
Isaiah: 1:17 118n2; 1:23 118n2; 33:17 87; 53 94; 53:2 94; 53:3–5 94; 53:5 94; 53:7–8 94; 53:10 94; 53:10–12 94; 53:12 94; 54:10 94
Isis 13–15, 23, 33
Israel 68–69, 80n1; abomination and 73; historical setting and the quest for 68–69; homosexuality 70; identity of 74; Leviticus and masculinity of men 69–75; man-to-man-sex 70; northern tradition 68–69; sexual intercourse with women 71; slave defends his masculinity 75–80

Jehu 68
Jeremiah: 22:3 118n2
Jesus Christ 124; clothing 36; crucifixion 93–94; gender journey 98; with Isaiah's servant of God 94; masculinity of 9; passing through genders 95–98; resurrection and exaltation 94; spiritual identification 99; suffering and death 99
Jewish wisdom-theology 96
John: 1:6 44; 1:35–40 82n14; 3:21 44; 13:23–25 82n14; 18:5–6 82n20; 18:15–6 82n14; 19:25–27 82n14; 19:34 98, 101n22; 20–24 82n14; 21:7 82n14
John Paul II, Pope 48n27
Joram 68

Joseph 76–80, 81n12, 82n19, 84; in Egypt 76; and Potiphar's wife 9
Josephus 36
Judah 68
Judges 19 72
Judith 119n10; 8:7 106, 108; 8:8 107; 8:10 118n7; 9:10 107, 109; 10:3 110; 10:3–4 108; 10:4 108; 11 110; 12:12–16 101n16, 110; 13 108; 13:4 109; 13:7 110; 13:8 110; 13:16 109; 14:1 110; 16:22 107; feminine public body 109; masculinity 107, 110; piety and sexual abstinence 107, 110; sexual purity 110; as single women 105–110; widow 106
Junge, Friedrich 65n2
Junia 38

Kantorowicz, Ernst H. 3–5
Khnum 21
1 Kings: 7:1–12 100n3; 10:4–22 100n3
King's Two Bodies, The (Kantorowicz) 3–4
Kügler, Joachim 47n20, 101n14, 102n23

Last Supper tradition 94
Levite's wife 72
Leviticus: 18–26 70; 18:1–5 73–74; 18:21 83n25; 18:22 70–71, 81n8; 20:13 70–71, 73, 81n9
Leviticus regulations 80n3
Lichtheim, Miriam 28n3, 64n1
Lings, K. Renato 80n2
Lohwasser, Angelika 118n3
Lot 71–72

ma'at 7, 14, 20
Maat-Ka-Ra 16, 19, 24
Make love, not war! 2
male-male sexual penetration 9, 50, 55, 60, 70, 72–73, 79

Index

male sexuality 7
male slaves 60
Manasseh 106
Mark: 5:27–30 36; 5:27–30 36; 10:45 94; 14:24 94
marriage 82n18; avoidance 9
Mary 43, 124
masculine domination 7, 12n5, 50, 53, 75, 117, 119n11, 120–121; body-sacrament 123; cultural framework 8, 26–27, 36–38, 49, 77, 86; exercise of 49; fight for 77; gender symbolism 95; and marriage 117–118; patterns of 86; system of 98
masculinity/masculinisation 42, 47n23, 61, 75, 105, 111; annihilation of 93; beauty 9, 87; beauty in Psalm 45 91; Christian women's public bodies 39; dominated Church 117; power 2, 71; public body 78; sexuality 55; singular 37; subordination 54; women's religious bodies 38
Matić, Uroš 64n1
Meier, John P. 48n28
Melaerts, Henri 46n16
men of Sodom 72
#MenToo-movement 2
Merkel, Angela 27, 31n27
Merz, Annette 114
#MeToo-movement 2
misogyny 10, 64, 76, 105
monogamy 58
Moses 101

naturalisation of feminine subordination 116
natural/mortal body 5–6
Neferura 14, 16, 26
Neils, Jenifer 46n16
Nero 36, 63–64
neuter singular 37

Nicholson, Paul 28n2, 44n1, 118n3
Nissinen, Martti 80n3
ntr nfr 91

Olson, Kelly 82n15
Omri 68
oriental god-king 63
orphan 103
Osiris 13–14, 28n4
Osiris (of) NN 33
otherness 75

Palette, Bull 65n6
Palette, Narmer 29n6, 51
Pastoral Letters 114
patriarchal gender-hierarchies 9
patriarchal marriage 9, 117
patriarchy 7
Paul (Apostle) 5–6, 8, 11n3, 34, 36, 38, 92; antiochian baptismal text 42; baptismal preaching in Corinth 41; gender policy 46n17; gender politics of today's churches 42–44
pederast relationships 55
pederasty 55
penetration 123
Pen-Nekhbet, Ahmose 26
perpetrators 99
Persian Empire 69
personal body 4–6
personal slavery 75
phallic aggression 72
pharaoh 28n1
Philippians: 2: 6–11 96–97
Philo 110–112, 119n15, 123
Phoebe 38
Plato 12n4
Platonism 7, 47n23
polygamy 59, 105
Potiphar 76–80
power hierarchy 81n5
praising asceticism 123

precarious identity 70
preeminent masculinity 58
pregnancy 54
private portion 97
prostitute 55
Proverbs: 17:2 83n22
Psalms: 45 89, 91, 94; 45:2–10 90; 45:3 87; 45:10–16 91; 45:17–18 90; 68:6 118n2
pseudo-Paul 117
Ptolemaic dynasty 44n2
public body 4–6, 29n10; masculinisation of 8
Punt, Jeremy 81n6

radical masculinisation of public body 19
Ramesses V 49
rape 49, 53; culture 1–3, 10, 49, 59; defeated enemy 60; effects of 54; gang rape 72; religio-historical patterns 2; in Rome 60; toxic-sacred trinity 3; *see also* masculine domination; violent sexuality
Re 14
Reaves, Jayme R. 102n23
Reinsberg, Carola 37, 59
Relief at Karnak *88*
religion 6
religion-based masculine domination 3
religious amulets 45n3
Roman Caesars 44n2
Roman Catholic Church 42–43, 47n24
Roman imperialism 60–61
Romans: 6:2–3 39; 6:7 11; 16:1 38; 16:6 46n19; 16:7 38; 16:12 46n19
romanticism 2
Rome: homosexual relations in 60; rape culture in 60; women in public sphere 60
Rößler-Köhler, Ursula 32

royal iconography 17, 20
Ryan, Scott C 101n13

sacrificial animal 94
salvation 44
Samaria 68
1 Samuel: 9:2 87; 16:12 87–88; 16:18 86–87; 17:42 87–88; 17:49–50 88; 18:20 82n17, 89; 27–28 82n17, 89; 28:13 101n12; 31:10 101n16
2 Samuel: 8:9–15 89; 11 89; 11:9 118n8; 13 77; 13:11 77; 14:25 87, 89; 14:26 89; 16:21–23 89; 16:22 118n8; 21:9–14 101n17
Saul, King 86–87
Scherer, Hildegard 46n19
Schipper, Bernd U. 69, 79
Schmitz, Barbara 119n10
Schreiber, Stefan 46n19
Schroer, Silvia 100n8
Sed festival 87
self-sacrificing slave 94
Seneca 67n29, 83n22
Septuagint 7
Seth 12n4, 49
sexual abuse 1, 10, 72, 87, 123; defending 122
sexual intercourse between men 9, 50, 55, 60, 70, 72–73, 83
sexualised violence 81n10
sexual(ity) 2–3, 89; act of penetration 53; aggression 72; behaviour 61; dangerous 123–124; ethics of 50, 124; freedom 76; global humanization 124; identity 55; integrity 1, 50, 78; intersection 6–8; male 7; object, male of lower status as 69–70; orientation 59; and power 7; regulations in Leviticus 79; revolution 2; rights 7; self-control 78, 80; sin 110; taboo 123; transgression 82n15;

violators 77; violence 1, 3, 49, 51, 121; violent ruler 51
sexual services 63; for slaves 60
shame 26, 40, 50, 62–63, 92–93, 95, 109, 121
shameful femininity 50
Shaw, Ian 28n2, 44n1, 118n3
Shepenupet I 104–105
short hair 41
sibling marriages 14
single women 105
Sinuhe 51–52
slave 55, 94
slave-form 97
slaveholder's wife 76
Smith, Mark 33, 45n4–5
social inferiority 70
Sodomites 81n7
Song of Solomon 84; 1:16 82n17, 85; 5:10–16 82n17, 85–86; celebration of human sexuality 86; erotic love 84; sociocultural echolon 85
son of the highest god Re 14
sons of God 6, 39–42, 94–95
sons of Israel 75–76
spiritual identification 99
Stavrianopoulou, Eftychia 46n16
Sternberg-el-Hotabi 45n7
Stiebert, Johanna 77
Stoa 7
stranger 103
strategic masculinisation 27
suckling scenes 118n4
Suetonius Tranquillus, C. 61–62
superior masculinity 120
supernatural/immortal body 5–6
survivors 99
sustainable development goals (SDGs) 121–122
swan-Zeus 58

tent Absalom 87–89, 118n8
Teresa of Avila 117

Thatcher, Margaret 27
Thebais 104
Theriomorphic depictions of king 65n5
Thutmose I 20–21, 23, 28
Thutmose II 14
Thutmose III 14–16, 18–19, 26
Tielesch, Simon 86
1 Timothy 114; 2:11–15 42; 2:12 116; 2:13 116; 2:14 116; 2:15 116; 5:3 115; 5:3–16 112–117; 5:5 115; 5:9 115; 5:11 115; 5:12 115; 5:14 116; 5:16 115
2 Timothy 114
Titus 114
Tombs, David 101n14, 102n23
toxic femininity 121
toxic masculinity 121
Trainor, Michael 102n23
transgenders 98
Trebilco, Paul R. 46n16
triumphator 67n24
Tsuji, Manabu 119n16
two bodies 3
Tyldesley, Joyce 26, 31n26

Uriah 118n8

Vestal Virgins 64
Veyne, Paul 118n1
victim blaming 50
violent sexuality 1–3, 49, 51–53, 55, 57, 59, 80, 81n10, 91, 121; ruler 51; Zeus syndrome 59
virginity 111
virgins 105, 111
Voderholzer 102n24
Vössing, Konrad 67n27

Wagener, Ulrike 114–115
widows 103–107
widows' tale 112–117
wife of Potiphar 76

Wilson, Stephen 100n6
women: belonging to Christ 112; sexual activity 117–118; singlehood 104

Yehud 69
YHWH-people 69, 74, 80n2, 100n10, 103
young "widows" promised to Christ 112–117

Zechariah 7:10 118n2
Zeus 3, 57–58, 120; masculinity 121; rapes Ganymede 59; sexual acts 58
Zeus syndrome 3, 66n19, 120–125; cost of 121; hierarchy of power 63; ignoring human and divine laws 60; reverberations of 64; seductions of 123; sexuality 123; violent sexuality 59

For Product Safety Concerns and Information please contact our EU representative GPSR@taylorandfrancis.com
Taylor & Francis Verlag GmbH, Kaufingerstraße 24, 80331 München, Germany

www.ingramcontent.com/pod-product-compliance
Lightning Source LLC
Chambersburg PA
CBHW051750230426
43670CB00012B/2222